MW01119700

Gender in Film and Video

Gender in Film and Video tracks changes in gender on screen by documenting trends of the internet age. This jargon-free book focuses on six instances of media in transition and their histories, including the rise of feminism on television, in sports events, and in comedy-drama series; the growth of DIY production by underrepresented groups through crowdfunding and YouTube channels; and struggles between fans and producers over control of casting and storytelling. This volume focuses on the breakdown of the categories (content, production, reception) that top-down production/distribution in TV and cinema tended to keep distinct. This text is for students in sociology, media studies, and women's and gender studies.

Neal King is Professor of Sociology at Virginia Tech. He has written two books on cinema: *Heroes in Hard Times* (Temple University Press 1999), which focuses on masculinity and intersecting relations of inequality, and *The Passion of the Christ* (Palgrave Macmillan 2011). He has also co-edited a volume on violent women in global cinema titled *Reel Knockouts* (University of Texas Press 2001). His research in inequality and popular media also appears in several anthologies as well as the *New Review of Film and Television Studies*, the *Journal of Film & Video*, *Postmodern Culture*, and *Gender & Society*.

Rayanne Streeter is a PhD student in Sociology at Virginia Tech. Her work has been featured in the *Women's Sport and Physical Activity Journal* and the *Oxford Research Encyclopedia of Crime, Media, and Popular Culture*. Her current research examines how body-positive media sites reconstruct health and womanhood.

Jessica Herling is a PhD student in Sociology at Virginia Tech. Her current research focuses on medical education about transgender health and sex/gender and representations of cellular aging in popular media.

Talitha Rose is a PhD student in Sociology at Virginia Tech. She has contributed to the *Oxford Research Encyclopedia of Crime, Media, and Popular Culture*. She researches women's production of diverse media, from feature filmmaking and online peer-to-peer communication, to craftivism.

Gender in Film and Video

**Neal King, Rayanne Streeter,
Jessica Herling, and Talitha Rose**

Routledge
Taylor & Francis Group

NEW YORK AND LONDON

First published 2019
by Routledge
711 Third Avenue, New York, NY 10017

and by Routledge
2 Park Square, Milton Park, Abingdon, Oxon, OX14 4RN

Routledge is an imprint of the Taylor & Francis Group, an informa business

Library of Congress Cataloging-in-Publication Data
A catalog record for this book has been requested

ISBN: 978-1-138-20623-6 (hbk)
ISBN: 978-1-138-20624-3 (pbk)
ISBN: 978-1-315-46549-4 (ebk)

Typeset in Adobe Caslon and Copperplate
by Apex CoVantage, LLC

CONTENTS

INTRODUCTION
GENDER IN FILM AND VIDEO

In the summer of 2017, *Wonder Woman* topped the global box office, surpassed hopes for its success, inspired women-only screenings in a theater chain, and pushed Patty Jenkins to the top ranks of American directors. Audiences enjoyed the film, the studio was relieved to see an entry in its franchise land with such a splash, and critics lauded the advancement that it portended for women in Hollywood. A month later, *Girls Trip* became the most successful adult comedy of the year in the U.S., drawing a cross-racial audience with its cast of black women who take the leads rather than the background roles they play in such fare as *Wonder Woman*. In October the same year, Hollywood exploded in pent-up recrimination as women across the industry broke a century of silence on sexual harassment and its perpetrators. The complaints came in numbers sufficient to unseat producers, directors, agents, and studio executives. We see in these three events examples of trends in the production of popular film and video, from which we can learn how race, gender, and other inequities work, and how industry dynamics shape their appearances on screen.

Consider the constraints under which women find Jenkins' kind of success. Her current, happy situation looks a lot like that of a white female forebear from a century ago. In 1917, Universal Pictures signed a distribution deal with the cinema writer/director Lois Weber, then one of the most powerful artists in Hollywood. (Her pro-birth-control movie *Where Are My Children?* was Universal's biggest hit of 1916.) A suffragette as well as hitmaker, Weber set up her own production company to make her movies independent of studio control, and submit finished products to them for distribution. Several decades later, Jenkins likewise made feminist movies her way, finding success in 2003 with her independently-produced *Monster*. That film starred feminist actress Charlize Theron as a sex worker driven to violence by men who prey upon such women. Jenkins drew offers of more movie projects from that success, and followed Weber in trying to make them outside of the control of the corporations that own major studios. Both women sought independence.

Both women failed. Weber lost her small production company when distributor Paramount grew unhappy with her film about men's mistreatment of women, *What Do Men Want?* By the early 1920s, major studios that owned theaters and could distribute movies widely were moving in the direction of factory-style control over production. They wanted less to do with mavericks like Weber and her sexually provocative moralizing about the place of women in our society, and began to push women into narrow niches as editors and 'script girls'. The men who owned those studios took over the movie-making business, and used their control over cinema chains to squeeze women out of the ranks of producers, writers, and directors. Weber directed a few more small pictures, but never had another hit, and fell out of the ranks of power players in those Hollywood studios (Stamp 2015). Women have directed few studio films since, and have found that they can achieve little success outside of that closed system.

Jenkins likewise saw her post-*Monster* indie films collapse for want of funding, and also withdrew to more minor projects. She speaks of having tried to make a version of *Wonder Woman* on her own, and also of having turned down an initial opportunity to help develop *Wonder Woman* for major studio Warner Bros. She continued to write her own scripts, but found no takers and worked in television instead. She tried to split the difference between doing it her way and working for a male-run studio when she signed on to direct another superhero-franchise sequel, *Thor: The Dark World*, in late 2011. (She received this opportunity in part because the feminist star of the franchise, Natalie Portman, had asked that a woman be allowed to direct such a big-budget installment and reap the rewards for her career.) Jenkins was to be the first woman to be given such a chance in the high profile and profitable comic-based genre. But she soon left that project over reported "creative differences," which is to say that the studio (Marvel, a smaller company since acquired by major studio Disney, which like Warner Bros is now one of the five studios in the Hollywood oligopoly making high-budget feature films in the U.S.) declined to support her version of the film and apparently fired her. They hired a man to direct it instead.

However, unlike Weber a century ago, Jenkins bounced back, in part by giving in. She joined this franchise-focused, major studio system rather than continue to buck its factory-production trend. After a decade of clashes between creators over its Wonder Woman property, including an unaired 2011 television pilot, Warner Bros returned to Jenkins in 2015, hiring her to helm its expensive film.

The toast of the town in summer of 2017, Jenkins had finally led a franchise blockbuster to success, on studio terms. She was hired only after star Gal Gadot had already been cast as the lead by another (male) director, chosen from the ranks of slender beauty queens. And though long committed to finding money to film her own scripts, Jenkins directed *Wonder Woman* from one written by a man to fit into a pre-established superhero franchise, which they have focused on such male heroes as Batman and Superman. Where Lois Weber would decline as a filmmaking force during the silent-movie era, Jenkins has risen to the top of blockbuster Hollywood by finding a place within a corporate system controlled almost entirely by white men (Figure 0.1).

Back in Lois Weber's day, no black women stood a chance of directing or starring in a Hollywood studio movie. A few made independent films during the 1920s, but none enjoyed corporate funding or wide distribution. Their work is largely gone, the film stock literally melted away. Indeed, as a white filmmaker, Weber

Figure 0.1 A superhero attacks in *Wonder Woman* (2017), directed by Patty Jenkins.

rose in the ranks in part through her production of racist movies about eugenics. Racism was still near its post-slavery peak, and
white-power backlash across the country stopped black political and
media-industry progress. The exclusion of black women from the
corporate production of film and video was nearly absolute for the
rest of the twentieth century. Even Jenkins' *Wonder Woman*, released
after a decade of open discussion of racist casting and storytelling
in Hollywood, remains focused on white characters, limiting black
performers to a few tough fighters and nurturing caregivers in the
background (Figure 0.2).

To counter this history of racial exclusion, the few black filmmakers who can gain wide release for their work tend to pay tribute
to their forebears. For instance, midway through Beyoncé's 2016
visual album *Lemonade*, she and other black women appear loung-
ing in the limbs of a massive tree, dressed in summer white. This
and other images from *Lemonade* echo a 1991 feature film by Julie
Dash, *Daughters of the Dust*, the epitome of feminist, independent
production by an outsider to the studio system. That film was also
the first ever directed by a black woman to gain wide release in the
United States.

Dash's film depicted her father's African American community on
the Sea Islands of the coast of South Carolina, at the turn of the
twentieth century. The oldest of her ancestors of that time could recall
slavery, and kept ahold of the West African culture of their ancestors.

Figure 0.2 Women of color appear onscreen in very little of *Wonder Woman*.

As a black woman, Dash told a story of such black history *for* black people:

> I really wanted to see an African-American historical drama that took me places that I had never been to before, just like I was taken places when I was watching foreign films or even some American epics. Films I was seeing at the time weren't really made for African-Americans—they were made to explain our history to others. . . . Usually, we're subject to films that have us in them—but they're explaining stuff to other people. We already know this information. We wanna see something that nourishes us.
>
> (Grierson 2016)

Dash approached Hollywood studios for support and found only rejection. She gained much of the small budget for her work from the government's Public Broadcasting Service instead.

As she filmed, Dash placed actors in a large tree in homage to an earlier Bill Gunn movie about black vampires, *Ganja and Hess* (1973) (Figure 0.3). That film had appeared during a brief window of opportunity for black filmmakers that had closed by the time Dash began to direct. (See Chapter 2 on the 'blaxploitation' cycles of the early 1970s.) And indeed no black woman directed any feature film given wide release in the U.S. until Dash screened *Daughters of the Dust* in 1991. A century after the invention of cinema, she appeared as a pioneer.

Figure 0.3 Three generations of homage between African American filmmakers: Bill Gunn's *Ganja and Hess* (1973), Julie Dash's *Daughters of the Dust* (1991), and Beyoncé's *Lemonade* (2016).

Operating from a larger base of capital resulting from her singing and dancing career, Beyoncé likewise focused independent productions on black culture (*Cadillac Records* 2008; *Obsessed* 2009), and hired a black woman to direct the former film. Neither enjoyed the massive success of her music and *Lemonade*.

Julie Dash was less fortunate and, like Patty Jenkins, saw her cinema career stagnate rather than rise after the success of *Daughters of the Dust*. She made several music videos and television films, but has yet to make another film for movie-theater screens and has not released a feature film in the twenty-first century, having turned down proposals for mainstream films in favor of projects focused on black women, which projects studios refused outright. Like Weber and Jenkins, Dash has paid a price for bucking a system that focuses feature films on the beauty of young white women and the muscular heroism of white men.

During those occasional times when studios release many black-themed films, they either result from bursts of independent financing (1970s blaxploitation and Tyler Perry's more recent Christian-themed romantic comedies) and/or from focus on violent crime (early 1990s 'hood/crack cycle). Neither gives much room to filmmakers like Dash to stage her historical dramas of black community. When Beyoncé restages scenes from Dash's film in her videos for *Lemonade*, she pays tribute to a black woman's voice not heard in cinemas for twenty-five years. Dash's work is a vital part of the history of black women in Hollywood, but that history is one of exclusion.

Still, recent trends in production appear to be opening up a new window of opportunity, which brings us back to the raunchy comedy *Girls Trip* (Figure 0.4). Since *Daughters of the Dust* hit cinemas in 1991, black women's films have seen wide release just once every few years: Kasi Lemmon's *Eve's Bayou* in 1997 (also quoted in Beyoncé's *Lemonade*), the beloved teen romance *Love & Basketball* in 2000, the kids Disney movie *Herbie Fully Loaded* in 2005, Beyoncé's production *Cadillac Records* in 2008. Of all movies given wide release in Hollywood, this means that black women direct about two per cent. Though

Figure 0.4 Black women front, center, and celebrating black culture in *Girls Trip* (2017).

this small number represents an expansion of opportunity over that of the 1970s and decades prior, the doors in Hollywood have remained largely closed.

However, this decade may be witness to a greater opening, with the success of such films as *Girls Trip*. Ava DuVernay has also found success with *Selma* (2014), the documentary *13th* (2016), and the chance to direct the Disney adaptation of *A Wrinkle in Time* (2018) with a multi-racial cast featuring a brown girl as the hero. DuVernay seems to be following the same corporate track as Jenkins has, ready to struggle for creative control: "I want to make films. And, if I can carve out my own vision, my own story from a corporate request—a great brand but not one that's particularly associated with black women—if I can bring some luxury and some beauty to the black female cinematic image through this job, I'm going to find a way to do that" (Martin and DuVernay 2014).

Nearly a dozen weeks after the release of the celebration of women's sexuality in *Girls Trip*, the *New York Times* and *New Yorker* magazine launched a series of long-suppressed, carefully reported accounts of sexual predation by powerful men in Hollywood that continues to grow and shake the industry as we write this book. A few men and dozens of women across the industry, including some of those named above, joined the chorus of complaints and are meeting in ad hoc groups to propose industry-wide shifts in policy designed to wrench open the doors that remained shut for so long.

In the chapters that follow we return to these protests against sexual abuse and the exclusion of women, to the constraints under which filmmakers such as DuVernay operate, and when opportunities for them open up or close again. We show how those trends generate both patterns in and public scandals over stereotyping vs. realism, appropriation vs. authenticity, exploitation vs. self-representation, and between the DIY spirit of YouTube and the $200 million blockbusters that can make women superstars on studio terms.

Theoretical Language

We next provide a vocabulary and outline by pitching the importance of gender and other inequalities such as race and sexuality in popular culture. By **film and video**, we mean any moving picture distributed to more than a few friends. We include everything from the feature cinema that formed in such places as Los Angeles back in Lois Weber's day, to the broadcast television that dates to the 1940s, to the programming on cable and video that arose in late 1970s, and to the explosion of DIY production via the internet at the end of the twentieth century. Today, popular video includes home-made confessions on obscure YouTube channels, such breakout cinema hits as *Girls Trip* and the independent black horror hit *Get Out* (2017), and the IMAX theaters that show such global hits as *Wonder Woman*.

We focus on film and video as **popular culture** and as vital to social life, rather than as mere trivia, because the rituals of sharing those with friends can charge them up with significance—coolness and buzz, with a kind of emotional energy that makes others want to see and talk about them, which turns those videos into currency. Groups adopt film and video as coins of their realms, as markers of belonging, as *their culture*. Familiarity with the stories popular in a group gives entrée to the banter, including such consumers in the daily streams of social life. By such word of mouth did *Daughters of the Dust* become a hit among urban black audiences in 1991 and among feminist scholars thereafter. A larger version of that event-status buzz drove *Lemonade* to set streaming records in 2016. The same contagion drives audiences to see *Wonder Woman* around the world and flock to *Girls Trip* weeks later. Some stories are more exclusive to smaller groups, while others reach global saturation. Either way, they can create a sense of import and emotional energy that drives social life. This is why we gather to watch games on television, stand in line to see summer hits in cinemas, and binge-watch TV series when pals gush about them in daily chatter. We forge friendships and other ties in part with our mundane talk focused on film and video.

For instance, the all-woman screenings of *Wonder Woman* in the U.S. in June 2017 left at least some of those who attended feeling in sync, as if in the solidarity of a powerful ritual:

> moviegoers reported that they had found themselves tearing up and laughing knowingly at the same points, and that with a crowd composed mostly of women, it seemed as if everyone was in it together
>
> (Buckley 2017).

This is the power of popular culture, to draw wide interest in the events, to forge ties between viewers and enhance the power of the groups included in it, to become currency. It achieves its importance by bonding people, by providing some of the glue in their friendships and organizations.

A different kind of contagion, one filled with greater rage, has led women to join the chorus of voices outing powerful men in Hollywood as serial abusers. After years of slow build-up of public accusations against famous men for years, a dam broke in October of 2017 when several women went on record with accusations of long-term harassment and assault by a prominent Hollywood producer. The flood that followed led to calls for systemic change to major-studio and talent-agency business models, and to the informal networking that men have used to demoralize, exploit, and exclude women in the business for a century.

Following that line of thought, we look at the role of popular culture in **inequality**. Mass media convey motion-picture stories in styles and languages that distinguish the groups both fluent and included in them from those who are not. Film and videos elevate some groups above others by featuring them in the stories they tell, by addressing their histories and concerns in ways familiar to them, while excluding others from the conversations. Some groups control the currency and others find themselves left out. By starring as heroes, the groups most often cast in those central roles become charged up with significance as well, as stars. At the center of mass attention and adoration, they become attractive and cool.

For instance, *Star Wars: Rogue One* (2016) featured Mexican and Asian men in major roles and a white woman as the star. Viewers from groups usually excluded from these franchises responded with joy at seeing people who looked like their kin on screen, as heroes in one of the most popular cycles in cinema history. Consider a viewer's anecdote from that film's release:

> On the second day of the new year, college student Perla Nation took her father to see *Rogue One*. A landscaper who immigrated from Mexico in the early 1980s, Pablo Perez doesn't pay much attention to Hollywood, whose activities on- and off-screen often seem worlds apart from his daily life. But as they sat in the darkened theater, Perez found himself transfixed—not just by the story and action unfolding onscreen, but in particular by one specific element.
>
> "When Diego Luna's character came onscreen and started speaking, my dad nudged me and said, 'He has a heavy accent,'" Nation, 27, wrote on her Tumblr page later that day. "When the film was over and we were walking to the car, he turns to me and says, 'Did you notice that he had an accent?'"

Perez couldn't shake his amazement that he had just seen a big Hollywood movie featuring a leading man who happened to sound like him. He grilled his daughter if this movie had made a lot of money. He questioned if it was popular. He wondered why Luna hadn't masked his accent. Nation told him about Luna's interviews, where he has declared pride in his natural Mexican accent.

And my dad was silent for a while and then he said, 'And he was a main character,'" Nation wrote. "And my dad was so happy."

In the Tumblr tags, Nation added that people have criticized her father's accent many times over the years. "I think this has really helped shift his outlook on it," she wrote.

(Sun 2017)

Rogue One also features a white female hero, which according to the film's director, owes to the fact that the screenwriter "has two daughters and he wanted to have a hero they could look up to" (Buchanan 2016).

Typically, Hollywood reserves such roles for actors who are white, male, able-bodied, cisgender, etc. Only on occasion, as in *Wonder Woman*, does it admit other groups to the fold of blockbuster heroes. But when it does, people long excluded from popular culture may feel themselves come into focus, and gain a measure of celebration.

These potential effects of video on our lives are matters of **inequality**, in which some groups are more likely than others to gain celebration as heroes or face exclusion and bear diminution or stigma as background players or victims of onscreen abuse. We focus our discussion of inequalities on **gender**, by which we mean everything that groups do to govern masculinity, femininity, and every combination or attitude toward those. We focus on gender because that relation of inequality organizes so much of our daily lives.

In Lois Weber's day, Victorian ideals of gender dichotomy reigned. Most people thought of each other as being strictly and permanently either boys or girls, growing up to be men and women, for life, and clearly indicating who was who in all situations. Employers gave most good jobs to men and had reserved nearly all political power for them, requiring that the sexes remain distinctly sorted and hoping that each man would marry one woman and support her with his wages. State laws forbade women dressing like men, in part for fear of women taking men's jobs, and outlawed all same-sex erotic contact. Retaining economic and political power, men could treat women as sexual property, currency in their relations with other men, by marrying off their daughters to the sons of other men, sharing sex workers at business events, and trading in sexual images of women in developing mass media. The sexual purity and attractiveness of marriageable white women was a valuable commodity. Other women often found themselves cast aside: underemployed, underpaid, and ignored in public.

Indeed, gender served as the basis for subordinating groups along other lines. The defense of white women's sexual purity was used to justify broad campaigns of lynching of African Americans; the promise to outvote immigrant groups helped (white) women's suffrage to pass. Ideals of white manhood still justified colonial invasions and harsh governance of restive slaves by Western militaries worldwide. Gender intersected with race, nation, sexuality, and class in more ways than we can document here, many of them resulting in forms of inequality that persist to this day. Though Lois Weber came to power during a wave of racially exclusive feminist action that resulted in white women gaining the ability to vote, she did so at a time when white men consolidated their control over such corporations as major Hollywood studios, preparing to exclude all women from executive positions for decades, including young white women as beautiful stars but relegating most other women to the margins of the industry. Only after another wave of feminist action, in the 1970s and 80s, did women begin to close some of those occupational gaps.

A century after the peak of Weber's career, medical and popular opinions of gender have changed, such that women are well over forty per cent of full time employees in the U.S., gay marriage is now legal in a growing number of nations, doctors less often rush to perform surgery on genitally ambiguous infants, and a growing number of people feel more comfortable with transitioning gender identities or refusing them altogether. Interracial marriage is now legal, though still a sensitive subject among many groups.

Even today, however, Hollywood remains a tough town for women who vie for the best jobs or for people who flout those ideals of natural sex and gender. Though young, white women still appear on screen in large numbers as attractive objects of men's pursuits, studios hire women to direct few feature films. Patty Jenkins is an exception; Julie Dash's experience is more common. Change has been slow, such that Hollywood is only beginning to experiment with gender-neutral acting awards, and over the objections of many women who note that the paucity of good roles offered even to white women means that gender neutrality in awards will further deprive them of support.

To account for these patterns in this book, we adopt a framework developed by black feminist scholars, the **intersectional** approach to women's and gender studies. Created to account for the exclusion of women of color and immigrants from social services and legal justice (Crenshaw 1989, 1991), intersectionality helps us to focus attention on the people left off screens and out of directors' chairs, and to see how accounts of their lives improve our theories of gender in film and video. When Hollywood filmmakers make movies about racial conflict, for instance, they most often tell stories of black men, as in last year's horror hit *Get Out*. When they focus on gender discrimination, they usually cast young, white actors, such as Charlize Theron, even in stories set in urban locations where people of color abound. As in Crenshaw's analysis, institutions such as courts of law ignore black women as too female to stand for blacks, too black to represent women. They are left out, either way.

The ranks of those unseen include trans women who find themselves portrayed by cismale actors on screen, lesbians and gay men usually played by straight actors, and the many women and people of color who must settle for criminal, girlfriend, and/or victim roles while white men play the heroes and most supporting roles besides. Old women, for instance, seldom appear on Hollywood screens. When Julie Dash cast 75-year-old actor Cora Lee Day as the Gullah matriarch in *Daughters of the Dust*, she broke unwritten Hollywood rules about the casting of leading roles. Cora Lee Day had played just a couple of small parts in films of the 1970s, during the blaxploitation cycle. In *Daughters of the Dust*, she is leader of the clan, bearer of the culture that binds members to each other as a source of strength. It's a compelling performance in an important part. Day never played another role of that significance. Old women have little to do in *Wonder Woman*, or *Girls Trip*, or most other feature films given wide release that year.

As we consider these exclusions, we focus on the roles of media organizations in them. Centuries of centralizing trends in production and governance include the formation of corporations, such as the major studios that make and distribute the world's most popular video, the conglomerates that control most theaters, cable channels, web servers, and other publishers. Even as wealth produced by such enterprise concentrates among the world's most privileged families, ancient inequalities have altered, giving some opportunities to various groups of women, sexual minorities, and people of color in terms of votes, time and spaces to organize, public voices, jobs, consumer options, and even starring roles as heroes. This is why women, especially women of color, must still fight for status and jobs in video production, and why they are slowly gaining both.

This centralizing trend toward corporate production has reversed in some ways over the twenty-first century, however, with the rise of the internet and smartphone use that foster peer-to-peer production and sharing of videos. Major studios once kept production of cinema and television distinct from consumption of it by fans and other viewers, by excluding such groups from any decision-making in Hollywood and other national film industries. The recent breakdown of such walls by the internet, the empowerment of fans to network online, and the ability for relatively poor people to use cheaper tools to make videos of their own are points of major focus in this book.

For instance, viewing of video and cinema has been shifting, from collective experiences in officially scheduled broadcast times at stadiums and/or cinemas, to a more personally controlled set of home and handheld viewings on the fly, streaming on impulse, and binge-watching alone or in groups. These new forms of consumption mix with the more established forms: shared watching of new episodes on network or cable TV timetables, and ritually-charged, centrally controlled blockbuster movie releases on cinema screens. People initially viewed Beyoncé's halftime Superbowl show *en masse*, live. They later streamed *Lemonade* mostly as individuals, on smaller devices. Some later made their own versions of her videos, just as so many parodied her riveting "Single Ladies" dance video with merrily inept remakes back in 2008.

Organization of the Book

A book so short on a topic so broad must pick its battles. We rely mainly upon data and examples from the U.S., in part because they are close at hand to us. This book is formed both of reviews of decades of scholarship and our own studies of genre-film development, public debate over media violence, YouTube celebrity and political debates, organized fandom and producer responses, televised athletics, and crowdfunding of feature films, all conducted in the U.S. and updated to reflect developments through early 2018 (e.g., Herling 2016; King 2008; King, Streeter, and Rose 2016; Rose 2015; Streeter 2016).

Gender in Hollywood video arises from a set of global relations that have given U.S. industries much capital to spend on their rapid development and tools to prevent the importing of "foreign" films, and thus limit the reach of most rivals. Though Thailand and India produce more movies than U.S. companies do, they have lacked the distribution to match Hollywood's reach (Scott 2004). Resistance to imperialism, rapid growth of national industries, and increasingly cross-national production have made Hollywood less insular and omnipotent than it once was (Kokas 2017), but its blockbuster model of franchise-film marketing and release and the massive export of English-language television continue to affect industries worldwide. We bear these relations in mind as we go but focus on English-language output mainly from North America.

Likewise, rather than provide comprehensive attention to every inequity that shapes gender on film and video, we focus on a few: race (especially black/white relations as described by the intersectional theory mentioned above), sexuality, and the rise to visibility of a population that challenges gender.

Chapter 1 charts a history of women's DIY culture, from riot grrrl punk to women's roller derby. The Women's Flat Track Roller Derby Association (WFTDA) has gone to great lengths to establish the feminist sport's athletic legitimacy despite stereotypes of women's contact sports. In this revival, television has become a touchy subject for skaters. They see it as a way to bring new audiences to their very physical and non-scripted bouts. But they guard against co-optation by centrally controlled sports media that trade more in sexual objectification and keeping women distinct from men than in the values of sporting toughness and physical courage that draw women to the bouts. The history of roller derby and its television broadcasts allow us to see how cycles of cultural renewal mix roles of consumer and producer, bringing amateurs into the television production process, sometimes as a defiant opposition to corporate routines, and sometimes in ways that leave them labeled inauthentic 'sell-outs'.

We show in Chapter 2 how white men built major studios in the West to limit competition and have used central control of distribution to resist the sorts of political calls for change that we see in 2017, in the global scandal over sexual harassment that erupted in Hollywood. Feature filmmakers from marginal groups look for ways to fund and broadcast their stories through independent channels. Pressured by corporate owners and given much discretion to use personal networks to limit risk, studio managers tend to give writing, producing, and directing jobs to people just like themselves: young, white cis men either closeted or straight. This chapter reviews a history of attempts to break this hiring mold. Employed by filmmakers like Julie Dash, crowdfunding has recently emerged as an alternative to corporate funding. When successful, it can allow creators to maintain control over small, first-time projects and is more likely than major studios to fund filmmakers and stories about protagonists who are female and/or LGBT. Such projects also include more political messages about issues such as race, sexuality, abortion, and misogyny, as seen in such 2014 crowdfunded crowd-pleasers as *Dear White People*, *Obvious Child*, and *A Girls Walks Home Alone at Night*.

We show in Chapter 3 how new channels of communication decentralized production streams, creating outlets for people with little money. DIY internet videos, such as those on YouTube, permit micro-celebrities to rake in millions of dollars by producing videos about their personal lives, often by using them to enter into public debate. As such, it creates the potential for a more democratic dialogue over social problems and changes than centrally controlled video such as Hollywood cinema has tended to provide. Many such videos celebrate nonstandard bodies and other gender transgressions, as well as feminism among other forms of activism, all alongside new forms of online misogyny. Women can complain of harassment and coercion of fans and other women by men in the YouTube community, framing their concerns over this "YouTube Abuse" in more or less feminist ways. The margins of centralized production foster oppositional culture.

We show in Chapter 4 how Western studios formed a century ago around racial and gendered storytelling, in which straight, white cis men lay claim to young, white women by rescuing them from the threats posed by other men. Groups not party to these contests play few roles. These constraints relax when production expands quickly enough to create a market for other heroes, or when producers find new ways to market directly to underserved groups. Many variants on the old white-boy-gets-the-white-girl storyline still amount to white-male fantasies and appropriations. We finish this chapter with the rise of new figures of black womanhood in popular video. Greater inclusion in production is key to the development of alternatives to the classical Hollywood storyline.

Chapter 5 shows how fans empowered by the shared DIY videos reviewed above can now intercede in the exclusions and misogyny of classical and blockbuster Hollywood. Major studios have long defended their business models in reply to such complaints, declaring their wares to be art free of politics or on the right side of history. These defenses have allowed white men running studios to continue to treat women with scorn and cast actors across national and racial types. Celebrity status being central to contemporary culture, the resulting stardom amounts to a scarce and precious resource and has drawn protest from underemployed, seldom-depicted, and long-degraded groups. Trade organizations and celebrities in competition for that public attention fight for inclusion in the system of production.

In Chapter 6, we show how fans embrace serial storytelling in popular video, and how producers harness that energy as a marketing tool. Fans use digital media to try to alter storylines of their favorite television shows, and are invited to do so by producers hoping to see them vouch to their friends for those products. We show how changing technologies and business models led to a wave of feminist television in the mid-2010s, including the Canadian science fiction show *Orphan Black*. As queer and feminist fans responded with anger to directions taken in the show, producers acceded to demands but defended their central control over major storylines. As in previous chapters, we find that industry business models, especially the degree of exclusive access to mass production, determine the look of gender on screen.

These studies are by no means comprehensive, as we pay less attention to many forms of inequality and popular video than they merit. We address neither music video, reality television, nor journalism. We pay little attention to inequalities in ability or body shape, religion, or age. Our point is not to provide encyclopedic coverage but to use a half dozen inquiries to touch on the major themes of feminist scholarship on film and video: the forces of intersecting inequalities on opportunities and popular imagery; public contests over stereotyping, objectification, fantasy, authenticity, and appropriation; and tensions between local and more central control of the means of production in a starkly unequal world. As lovers of video and critics of all barriers to participation in making it, we treat these forms of popular culture as vital to the organization of our unequal worlds.

References

Buchanan, Kyle. 2016. "*Rogue One* Director Gareth Edwards on Diversity, Reshoots, and That *Star Wars* X-Factor": *Slate.com*. Retrieved June 10, 2017 (www.slate.com/blogs/browbeat/2016/12/12/rogue_one_director_gareth_edwards_on_diversity_reshoots_and_the_appeal_of.html).

Buckley, Cara. 2017. "Solidarity at an All-Female Screening of *Wonder Woman*": *The New York Times*. Retrieved June 10, 2017 (www.nytimes.com/2017/06/05/movies/wonder-woman-all-female-screening.html).

Crenshaw, Kimberle. 1989. "Demarginalizing the Intersection of Race and Sex: A Black Feminist Critique of Antidiscrimination Doctrine, Feminist Theory and Antiracist Politics." *University of Chicago Legal Forum* 1989:139–68.

Crenshaw, Kimberle. 1991. "Mapping the Margins: Intersectionality, Identity Politics, and Violence against Women of Color." *Stanford Law Review* 43(6):1241–99.

Grierson, Tim. 2016. "Daughters of the Dust: Why the Movie That Inspired Lemonade Is Back": *Rolling Stone*. Retrieved June 10, 2017 (www.rollingstone.com/movies/features/why-we-need-indie-movie-daughters-of-the-dust-right-now-w450955).

Herling, Jessica Lauren. 2016. "Online Community Response to Youtube Abuse." Master's Thesis, Sociology, Virginia Tech, Blacksburg, VA.

King, Neal. 2008. "Generic Womanhood: Gendered Depictions in Cop Action Cinema." *Gender & Society* 22(2):238–60.

King, Neal, Rayanne Streeter and Talitha Rose. 2016. "Cultural Studies Approaches to the Study of Crime in Film and on Television." in *Oxford Encyclopedia of Crime, Media, and Popular Culture*, Vol. 1, edited by N. Rafter. New York: Oxford University Press.

Kokas, Aynne. 2017. *Hollywood Made in China*. Berkeley: University of California Press.

Martin, Michael T and Ava DuVernay. 2014. "Conversations with Ava DuVernay: 'A Call to Action': Organizing Principles of an Activist Cinematic Practice." *Black Camera* 6(1):57–91.

Rose, Talitha Kanika. 2015. "Funding Female Features: Crowdfunding for Gender Equity in the Film Industry." Master's Thesis, Sociology, Virginia Tech, Blacksburg, VA.

Scott, Allen. 2004. "Hollywood and the World: The Geography of Motion-Picture Distribution and Marketing." *Review of International Political Economy* 11(1): 33–61.

Stamp, Shelley. 2015. *Lois Weber in Early Hollywood.* Berkeley: University of California Press.

Streeter, Rayanne. 2016. "Roller Derby as a Site of Resistance: Strategies for Countering Sexist and Homophobic Assumptions in Women's Sports." *Women in Sport and Physical Activity Journal* 24(2):143–51.

Sun, Rebecca. 2017. "Rogue One: How Diego Luna's Accent Gave a Voice to a New Set of Fans": *The Hollywood Reporter.* Retrieved June, 2017 (www.hollywoodreporter.com/heat-vision/rogue-one-diego-lunas-accent-gave-a-voice-a-new-set-fans-961343).

1

DIY REBELLIONS AND THE PERILS OF SELLING OUT

New recruits to roller derby often tell the older players how they heard about the sport. Many have said that they saw it on a flyer, read a story in the news, or know someone who played; but, soon after its 2009 release, the answer was often "*Whip It*," a popular film written by a skater and directed by Hollywood feminist Drew Barrymore. Veterans might groan in annoyance at seeing the game they boosted as a real sport co-opted by yet more fiction. The campy license taken by *Whip It* in its depiction made it fun to watch and drew new fans and skaters. But women who had played for years remained wary of the mass-media images that featured more spectacle than sport, more off-track drama and breaking of rules than focused competition among athletes. Skaters, particularly those in the Detroit area where the movie was shot, were featured in the movie and helped to train the stars, but had little control over the image that it painted. A major studio (Fox Entertainment, owner of the century-old studio Twentieth Century Fox) had funded a feminist filmmaker to tell a story of their sport that was easy to market to a broad audience as a family-friendly rebellion, even as it traded in the stereotypes of women's melodrama and undisciplined clowning during the games that skaters have resisted since its revival.

The Women's Flat Track Derby Association (WFTDA), as governing body of the sport, advised teams how best to use *Whip It*:

"This is a great opportunity for us to take advantage of the popularity the movie will bring. We want to make sure we are ready for the popularity when it comes" (Loca 2007). WFTDA encouraged teams to be in contact with studio Fox Searchlight, to be a part of Barrymore's press tour, and to align themselves with local theaters to promote their leagues on opening day. WFTDA recognized that the film could encourage old myths about roller derby and sought to give leagues the tools to answer "undesirable questions" in ways that separated the major-studio fiction of *Whip It* from the largely DIY ('do it yourself') sport. WFTDA posted a FAQ page addressing such questions as "I bet you throw a lot of elbows, right?", "Is roller derby real?", and "I used to love watching roller derby on TV! Is it like that?" (WFTDA 2007). The desire to prep for such questions stems from roller derby's long history of co-optation from mainstream elements that have sought to make money off the image of the roller derby girl.

Further co-optation threatened when Hot Topic, an American chain specializing in counterculture-related apparel, released a line to tie-in to the film: "You won't have to battle it out on the rink to sport some killer Roller Derby fashion. It's all right here. So grab your girls, get dolled up and take your victory lap!" In their memoir and player's guide to roller derby, Jennifer "Kasey Bomber" Barbee and Alex "Axles of Evil" Cohen told readers that "We dread that derby has jumped the proverbial shark when the national retail outlet Hot Topic launches a 'Roller Derby Queen' line featuring photos of bruise-free models and not a single skate in sight" (2010:222). The once oppositional nature of roller derby seemed to have been appropriated by mainstream merchants and reduced to baubles more easily sold to more girls than would ever commit to feminist defiance.

The punk-rock riot grrrl movement had been through a similar co-optation and diminishment in the 1990s. And other sports battled television networks over damage to their rebel images and communities: snowboarding, skateboarding, and BMX. We focus on these struggles over women's DIY, outlaw status on video because roller derby players followed other rebels in making space for women and girls to flout gender constraints, defy rules that constrain them, take charge of their business, and to do so in industries that had long kept men in the center of focus. Roller derby's DIY feminism and power to open opportunities for young women risked becoming lost when co-opted and commercialized by various mass-culture media, which could happen all the more quickly when skaters invite said media to provide wider platforms for the sport. Using participant observation, interviews with skaters, and analysis of roller derby forums and websites, we show how the sport flouts gendered myths of women's athletics and opens opportunities, and how the women maintain their authenticity as competitive players, even as they pursue legitimacy through broadcast and financial success on ESPN.

Cultural Cycles

Co-optation of a rebellious, DIY scene like roller derby to the dollar-focused salesmanship of mass consumer culture is nothing new. Sociologists have long noticed that unruly and moralistic groups, who work to build utopias or at least shrink from the corruptions around them, make high demands on their members. Few find it easy to reject mainstream life and sustain that resistance for long. Over time, most such groups either stay too small to have much effect, lose their members and fall apart, or grow by reducing their demands and succumb to the materialist world they had meant to reject. And those that grow by returning to mainstream life may alienate the most demanding of their members, prompting those to split off to form new rebellions, and so on. This cycle ensures both that moral campaigns give in to the very forces they protest and that new ones will always arise.[1]

Entertainment firms can hasten this cycle in realms of music, sports, and other pastimes, by encouraging accommodations with marketing muscle and offers of contracts to players. For instance, Dick Hebdige studied subcultures, such as punks, that flaunt their rebellion in terms of clothing, music, and other expressions sold as consumer items. He found that record companies look for wares to sell and audiences to buy. They may begin with such rebels as offensive punk rockers or other anti-capitalist musicians, who scorn mainstream consumers but who provide styles that can become trendy if marketed well. Despite the mutual hostilities that keep rebels to the fringe, corporations see opportunity on the rise:

> [A]s the subculture begins to strike its own eminently market- able pose, as its vocabulary (both visual and verbal) becomes more and more familiar, . . . the mods, the punks, the glitter rockers can be incorporated, brought back into life, located on the preferred map.
>
> (Hebdige 1979:93–4)

Within a couple of years of the movement's rebellion against bour- geois consumerism, fashion magazines sported punk looks, with ads that promised that "To shock is chic" (96).

Merchants court such rebels when they can sell more directly to diverse groups, rather than through narrow channels of distribution to a mass market with low tolerance for defiance. For instance, by the mid-1950s, a handful of networks dominated television (TV, for short) broadcasting in the U.S., constrained by limited band- width of over-the-air signals. The corporations that owned those networks standardized TV fare in an attempt to address the larg- est consumer groups: white middle-class women, men, and their children. By contrast, producers of video now enjoy wide access to consumers through many media and can avoid the homogenizing effect of single-medium, mass distribution. They can exploit diverse niches rather than always seek lowest common denominators of the viewing population. In this new context, of more direct narrowcast- ing to niche markets, TV programming has become a rich source of innovation and diversity on screen and off, including much politi- cal challenge that the big three networks had so long forbidden (to which we return in Chapter 6).

Sports TV has been shaped by these trends. The first airing in the early days of TV drew in impressive viewership. With original pro- gramming still sparse, and roller derby easy to film and theatrically interesting, the new network ABC began to plug bouts into every time slot. Several other networks also experimented with the sport, in the relatively open competition of those early days. By 1950, roller derby aired up to five times a week in some regions. But viewership remained unreliable, and ABC took it off the air in 1951.

Roller derby would return to TV in the 1970s, by which time major network coverage of women's sports had narrowed in favor of the sports played by men. Aimed at a mass audience, the closed system of production had pushed female athletes mostly to TV's sidelines, treating them more as characters than as athletes. To improve derby's appeal to TV audiences, producers scripted storylines, chose winners of bouts, orchestrated fights, stylized flashier outfits, and emphasized the personas of skaters. But none of the increasingly gaudy attempts at TV revival, repeated about once per decade over the rest of the century, would last very long.

The proliferation of sports outlets in the cable and streaming eras, as channels grew in number from dozens to hundreds, appears to have reopened possibilities for the now feminist sport. The increasingly open system of production uses rather than refuses innovation, seeking to satisfy diverse smaller markets, opening up for local rebel scenes the possibility of going professional, albeit at risk of "selling out" in the cultural cycle. And roller derby shares this feminist-on-the-fringe-of-stardom niche with the punk rock of riot grrrl, such that the industrial context from which riot grrrl emerged helps to explain how they have both moved through this cycle.

The popular music industry was opening, as TV would later do, by the early 1980s. Record companies with diverse but racially segregated catalogues of artists used new distribution methods to gain direct access to specialty record stores. No longer constrained by middle-men who narrowed the channels of distribution and kept racial groups of musicians segregated, record companies could stock large record stores with far greater assortments of artists and music (Lopes 1992). As a result, many buyers were able to shift toward gender and racial diversity in the acts they patronized, which expanded the overtly leftist, queer, and feminist art that could gain popularity. Politically charged hip-hop began its rise to a dominance that would cross the older lines of segregation. New technologies and business models had opened doors long shut to marginal groups.

In this new context, underground and rebellious acts could gain wider popularity if they were willing to play by the rules of marketing departments of the record companies. To work on the fringes of entertainment, to make little money and enjoy little rest, is a demanding lifestyle. Players might wish for higher pay and the greater exposure that goes with it. Bands and teams hoping to recruit must lower their demands by raising the rewards of the rebellion. But growing can also diminish the substance of that defiance, alienating those who joined in the first place. Strong feminists may abandon roller derby, just as punk fans may dismiss a band, as having sold out. They seek newer, more local, and 'authentic' scenes, because of the way in which the MTVs and ESPNs open up to include them. So the cultural cycle goes.

Riot Grrrl Cycle

As rebel scenes, roller derby and the 1990s punk-rock offshoot riot grrrl share the DIY ethos that women should take control of production, that they should tell stories that the mainstream ignores, and that they should defy sexism in their respective fields (Pavlidis 2012). Some of the first skaters of the derby revival had been part of riot grrrl music scene, and much of the defiant style of the sport has derived from that scene. These links between roller derby and riot grrrl make co-optation of the latter bode ill for the former's future. Having reviewed the conditions under which mass media industries either exclude rebellion when closed, or turn it into commodities when open, we now look more closely at the recent histories of these two rebellions that have put feminists on video.

Emerging from white and often gay independent publishing and punk rock scenes in Washington state, the name adapted from a reference to urban race riots, riot grrrl was a white grassroots music scene committed to feminist empowerment of girls, to make music of their own and not merely support the men around them

(Schilt 2003). Music undergrounds tend to be racially segregated, hip-hop undergrounds including blacks more than whites (Harrison 2009), and punk doing the opposite. Riot grrrl appears to have remained as white as the scene from which it emerged, and maintained its whiteness in part by drawing its name from a race riot without commenting on the race in the riot (Nguyen 2012). The very unremarked nature of race suggests to us the usually undiscussed whiteness of the scene.

Riot grrrl otherwise pushed up against the status quo and engaged in disalienation, putting women and their stories at the forefront through the production and distribution of music, zines, and TV shows focused on women's issues including rape, sexuality, and health. Women called their punk bands Bikini Kill, Bratmobile, Heavens to Betsy, and the like, and steered their lyrics away from heterosexual relationships, mocked stereotypes of womanhood, and defied the ways women learn to hate themselves. In "Rebel Girl," Bikini Kill sing "When she talks, I hear the revolution/In her hips, there's revolutions/When she walks, the revolution's coming/In her kiss, I taste the revolution." The ode to feminist solidarity includes the erotic, and though the lyrics are not more dramatic than typical pop and rock, it departs from depictions of girls' ties to each other as catty, romance as heterosexual, and other problems as immaterial. Kathleen Hanna, former singer for the band, explains:

> We have to sit through so much music about being in love or breaking up, and that is some of the most irrelevant shit out there. Not having health care and having a bladder infection I couldn't get treatment for; I think I cried over that more than I cried over any guy. Where are the songs about being broke or our friends' being broke?
>
> (quoted in Riordan 2001:287)

To bolster their lyrics, performers scrawled "SLUT" and "BITCH" across their bodies with permanent markers for shows. They dismissed mass culture by singing of lives outside of celebrity circles.

Although riot grrrl held promise, to record companies, as a commodity, it refused the production values to which paying listeners had grown accustomed, scorned consumer marketing, and often flouted a sexual deviance still illegal in many states at the time. In such cases, as part of the cultural cycle, a scene may address itself to a larger audience, or see its appropriation without its cooperation, in ways that restrain its insolence, translate obscenities and calls to crime into radio-friendly lyrics and objects easily worn in daily life, and groom its outright rejection of consumer capitalism and legal family structure into mere teasing and cheek. For riot grrrl, this meant seeing record companies trivialize the movement's anti-capitalist and pro-lesbian-feminist demands by remarketing girl power, once its rallying cry, as the less threatening Spice Girls and the "angry women in rock" of the mid 1990s (Strong 2011). Although women marketed under the latter rubric, such as Alanis Morissette and Fiona Apple, sang about some of the issues that riot grrrl had chosen, they did so in recordings that sounded and looked like expensive studio productions rather than the grainy video and yard-equipment roars of DIY punk shows. Retailers refashioned riot grrrl style by selling expensive Doc Marten boots, leaving unspoken the street-fighting history of punk and the queer bashing and sexual assaults that so many riot grrrls had confronted. Articles in *Seventeen*, *Spin*, and *Rolling Stone* often misquoted riot grrrls, portrayed its members as sex objects, and downplayed their calls for queer and anti-consumer revolution.

To combat this co-optation, some riot grrrls attempted a "media blackout" by refusing to speak to reporters, who replied with even more widely inaccurate stories, leading to rifts within the movement between those who gave interviews and those content to withdraw from the mainstream (Riordan 2001). As Bleyer (2004:51) explains:

> the entire zine movement was effectively over, one could say, almost as soon as it began, having been swallowed up by the great maw of popular culture with dollar signs flashing in its eyes. Like hip-hop, grunge, and punk rock, the language style of riot grrrl were absorbed, repackaged, and marketed back to us in the most superficial form of its origin.

Media Meets Sports

The reproduction of men's domination over women in sports is not unlike that found in other areas of culture, including the films explored later in this book. Research has demonstrated that organized team sports, as integrated into public schooling and town life in the nineteenth century, were invented literally to separate white men from everyone else, lauding the former as superior athletes and restricting women's participation categorically (Kimmel 1994). Games served as rituals, with solemn, nationalist elements that celebrated white boyhood and manhood. A century and a half later, professional athletics are almost entirely segregated by sex and hostile toward openly gay athletes. Race continues to structure the leadership of sports, from the quarterbacking of football to the coaching of teams. Sporting rituals celebrate the importance and emotional excitement of boys and men hitting and pushing each other, and demonstrating a strength lauded as unique to their sex, while girls and women are seen as either unable to play or as odd should they do the same (Messner 2010).

Though the number of women in sports has increased since the passage of Title IX in the U.S., men continue to play at higher rates and at higher levels than women, and hold more positions of power in sports organizations (i.e. coaching, managers, owners, etc.). Mainstream venues and media continue to treat women's sports as relatively trivial. Because contact sport has been defined as a male space and clearly continues to be occupied by men, many view women who play contact sports as invaders and threats to the status quo. Female athletes face sexual stigma and stereotyping that discredit their athletic professionalism (Blinde and Taub 1992).

As part of this dismissal of women's athletics and the maintenance of it as men's turf, the coverage of women's sports on TV news remains low. ESPN's *SportsCenter* gave but two per cent of its hour-long highlight show to the topic in 2014 (Cooky, Messner, and Musto 2015). That researcher found that, of 14 hours of coverage, men's sports received 13 hours, gender-neutral sports just over 20 minutes, and women's sports just 17 minutes of broadcast time. Live coverage of men's sports far outweighs that of women's, with men receiving primetime slots and channels. Announcers call men's games with more enthusiasm. Journalists frame their coverage on women's appearances, marital status, and their lives as mothers while ignoring their athletic accomplishments. For example, in their analysis of media portrayals of women's Olympic beach volleyball players, Sailors, Teetzel, and Weaving (2012) found that players were represented as either mothers or sexual objects. Finally, sports besides the "big three" (i.e. basketball, football, and baseball) are also treated marginally, receiving little news and live coverage and relegated to lesser channels or online platforms.

Other alternative sports, also known as extreme or lifestyle sports, have developed in opposition to the traditional, rule-bound, competitive, and consumeristic sports through similar grassroots and DIY efforts. For example, snowboarding gained popularity in the 1980s in direct opposition to skiing which snowboarders saw as overly regimented, expensive, and bourgeois (Heino 2000). Snowboarders developed a counter-culture that differentiated itself through style, language, and an anti-establishment attitude. Rather than tight-fitting neon colored clothes typical of skiers at that time, snowboarders drew from youth grunge and hip-hop styles adopting baggy, brown-colored clothes that looked like they could have come out of any working man's closet. They decorated snowboards and supported rivals to favor personal ties and style over professional uniformity and competitiveness. After competing with enthusiasm, snowboarders would present a roll of duct tape as the Golden Duct Tape trophy, mocking the solemnity of the profession. They disdained the hierarchical and profit-driven and championed instead a DIY ethos where the members maintained expertise and control without need of governing officials or corporate sponsors.

However, many of these sports, despite attempts not to "sellout," have submitted their sports to the same type of co-optation seen in riot grrrl. As Wheaton (2010:1058) explains:

> The allure and excitement of lifestyle sport has been appropriated to sell every kind of product and service imaginable, from cars and deodorant to holidays, and to market geographic regions. Lifestyle sports have been the focus of numerous 'mainstream'

television shows and films such as *Blue Crush*, *Point Break*, *Kids*, *Jackass*, *Touching the Void*, and *Dogtown* and *Z-Boys*. . . . The media's appetite for such sports is exemplified by the continued and still-growing success of ESPN's X Games.

Like the Roller Derby Queen line and riot grrrl before that, the style of skateboarders, snowboarders, surfers, and the like have been mass marketed and sold to non-members. Anyone can buy a pair of DC Shoes without embedding themselves in the skateboarding culture. And, as TV and corporate sponsors identified alternative sports as a way to tap into the young male market, they used images of these athletes to sell products both related and unrelated to their sport. Still, the major point of co-optation and commercialization came with the induction of ESPN's X Games.

The X Games were founded in 1995 by ESPN (owned by ABC, itself a division of The Walt Disney Company) and backed by a transnational set of corporate sponsors who sought to capture the lucrative youth market. In doing so, the X Games brought alternative sports to a wider audience, instituted a competition style of play where snowboarders, skateboarders, and BMX riders competed for medals and prize money, and became the ultimate forum for setting records and performing more technical and creative maneuvers for international audiences. However, in televising these sports to a wider audience, they undid much of their oppositional nature. Pointed camaraderie turned to individualist competitiveness, and anti-capitalism turned to the search for advertising sponsorship (Edwards and Corte 2010; Thorpe and Wheaton 2011). Like riot grrrl, many of these alternative sports reached more potential members, in hopes of spreading their defiant views, but their original messages go by the wayside as the price of that wider reach.

Roller Derby and ESPN

As we saw above, skaters are not naïve to the problems of televised women's sports and alternative sports. They know their sport's own torrid history of being groomed to fit mass culture prior to the revival that began in 2001 in Austin, Texas. This was a grassroots feminist organization by women, for women, which has grown from one league in 2001 to over 400 worldwide in 2017. Women's flat track roller derby remains largely DIY, as skaters developed it from the ground up through trial and error and continue to adapt it to this day. All aspects of the sport are discussed among members in online forums, in practices, and in league meetings, and are voted on by skaters, unlike professional sports regulated by centralized leagues run by owners of teams and corporate heads. Skaters advertise their own bouts, they lay down the court to skate on, and they provide every bit of equipment and legal permission needed to play. As WFTDA's governing philosophy states, roller derby is "by the skaters, for the skaters."

Although roller derby has the training, regulations, and physical consequences of team contact sports, and retains the whiteness of its riot grrrl roots, it has also kept some of the spectacle of its former television days, with derby names and boutfits as means of a gendered defiance. Derby names are pseudonyms under which players skate, often vulgar puns on other bits of popular culture: Sara Problem, Clitty Clitty Bang Bang. Boutfits are their uniforms, modified to play up derby names and offer cheeky defiance. Many were hypersexualized over the decades, featuring fishnets and short skirts, lacking much padding and protection from injury (Gieseler 2014). As skaters have sought to professionalize the sport, they have often opted to do away with boutfits in favor of traditional uniforms, becoming less rebellious and more professional, less a mockery of the industry and more a part of it. But this has been a point of contention among some skaters who feel that getting rid of boutfits, rather than keeping them, now counts as selling out (Streeter 2016). Such political debate is typical of roller derby, a contact sport that draws upon stereotypical masculine behavior while focused on and owned by women. The defiance of gender resulted in the 2016 Gender Statement:

> An individual who identifies as a trans woman, intersex woman, and/or gender expansive may skate with a WFTDA charter

team if women's flat track roller derby is the version and composition of roller derby with which they most closely identify.

(WFTDA 2016)

Such politics remain controversial in mainstream culture worldwide, such that the next move toward TV would be more fraught than any before, raising the same questions about selling out their sexual deviance and feminism that the riot grrrls who inspired them had faced. The movement of women into mainstream video could very well lead to a "sell-out" that would cause the most demanding women to quit in disgust and look for some new rebellion to DIY.

Besides the short lived A&E docu-series *Rollergirls* (Kearney 2011) and the long list of fictional movies and TV shows that depict roller derby (e.g., *Whip It* 2009; *The Fosters* 2013–; *Kansas City Bombers* 1972), skaters are mostly weary of television, based on the experiences described above. As skaters explain in interviews conducted by author Streeter:

> typically when you talk to somebody about roller derby and they don't know what it is they always assume it was how it was in the '70s, like when they would watch Raquel Welch movies. . . . So, I think there's an element that it's not taken seriously as a sport, because in the past it wasn't really a serious sport. And that's where a lot of people kind of think "that's how it is."

> I feel like it's a lot of education of people to what roller derby looks like now. It's a completely different sport than what we had back in the 70s, but that's what people typically will think of is the 70s where it's roller girls . . . beating each other up for entertainment.

> I mean everybody's seen *Whip It* and *RollerJam* so they assume that you use your fists, that you can elbow people, and so I think definitely educating people about the game and how it works right now and the rules.

Skaters speak of difficulties in being taken seriously as a sport today in the wake of the older images, while they recognize the importance of TV as a way to legitimize it as a profession. Before the advent of

ESPN, many voiced uncertainty about corporate television, seeing its benefits but also the compromises that it would demand of their DIY approach. Tonya[2] argues that:

> one of the biggest problems that's going to face derby, as far as being a professional sport, is the fact that it is so grassroots and it is so do-it-yourself, and that's what makes it great . . . we put our blood, sweat, and tears, time, money, energy, emotions, we put everything into this and we build it . . . and we want to control it. But, in order to be on a professional level, that's when you have to open your door to corporate sponsors and owners and coaches. And most of the time people aren't going to put their money in something they can't control.

Control matters to skaters who have seen the results of ceding to television before, not only in derby but also in other sports. Snowboarders became professionals by relying more heavily on sponsors in exchange for control over their content (Coates, Clayton, and Humberstone 2010). Skaters hope to give up less, perhaps in exchange for less. As one high-ranking member of WFTDA put it, "For WFTDA, the main priority is that skaters retain control over the sport and have a hand in shaping the game and how it is played." Tara describes the balance that she would accept:

> Derby represents a grassroots mentality right now, and "pro" denotes a commercialization of the sport that we tend to shy away from. We like the term "legitimate" sport, and that's something we're working really hard to- making it recognizable and semi-pro, but I don't think we would move to a model where we are owned by somebody or paid by somebody.

Brooke likewise sees a potential compromise:

> I'm not sure that anybody in roller derby is willing to let go of the control in order to allow us to be paid to play. I think that's

the big factor, and I'm definitely not comfortable saying "Yeah, pay me, but that means that you get to make all the decisions."

Skaters voice ways to sacrifice some of derby's unique qualities, to align with what they see as authentic competitive athletics on TV. They could, for instance, limit their more expressive behavior. Nancy explains,

> there definitely is a kind of discussion, rumblings throughout the derby community about if we want to move forward towards our goal of bringing derby to the forefront as a legitimate sport and work towards going to the Olympics and getting, you know, huge corporate sponsors, being on TV, that- There is a push for people to say, "let's step back and maybe take that derby name out of it and go back to being last names and being real people and being real athletes as opposed to a persona."

There is a feeling that derby names hold roller derby back from gaining legitimacy. In a blog post, Ginger Snap, a skater for Gotham Girls Roller Derby, relayed a similar sentiment:

> So . . . we want to take this sport to the next level? We want to be on ESPN? We want to be in the Olympics? How do you think we are going to get there with names like "Clitler" and do you think Fox Sports is going to want to touch us when they hear that a skater's name will always have to be censored like we've already seen with Clitty Clitty Bang Bang . . . But if we want to take it to the next level it's hard to justify these names. These names say that we don't take our own sport seriously enough even to be PG-13 and accessible to all the aspiring junior derby girls—our little derby sisters—out there.
>
> (Snap 2011)

A west coast skater, Maggie, agrees: "with that you can't really have names like, you know, MuffDiver. People aren't gonna want to see that on ESPN."

Other skaters, such as Gigi, focus on outfits and the potential for becoming more uniform and focused on instrumental athletic competition rather than vibrant rebellion:

> My first couple years with the team everybody wore freaky outfits . . . like big, tall socks with things on them, like skull and cross bones. A lot of people don't wear those anymore on my team, but the first couple years I was playing everybody wore them . . . I think a lot of teams are trying to get away from that I think 'cause . . . legitimate sports don't do that.

By eliminating the more personal and defiant, to be like traditional sports and be televised, roller derby is giving up one way in which they transgressed and pushed against mass corporate culture and the constriction of women's appearances in public. Greater legitimacy as athletes means less defiance. Women struggle with the prospect of adapting to the men's model of sport that they took such pride in flouting.

Their coverage by ESPN in 2015 and 2016 was limited to a few games on ESPN streaming service. WFTDA hired the production company that shot the games; and, though held to ESPN standards, the TV production looked much like what had aired on WFTDA.tv before: the same sponsors, announcers, and graphics, if a little more polished and now branded with ESPN rather than WFTDA. One of the skaters to whom we spoke linked this to their DIY ethos, explaining, "By generating this product in-house, we retain control over the image and assets so they can be distributed in a way that respects the skaters and positively promotes roller derby at every level. The WFTDA is 'for the skaters, by the skaters,' and this endeavor reflects that mission."

For a bout streamed in November 2015, athletes wore matching jerseys and helmets, though the bottoms varied from small shorts to long pants, mostly tight and all black. Because television by ESPN attains the height of legitimacy, it makes sense to skaters to dress in uniform manner. Still, Scald Eagle of the Rose City Rollers kept her signature face paint for the televised bout, along with her American-flag patterned skates. ESPN broadcast some derby names, but appears to have drawn a line at sexual allusions. The network listed Licker N' Split, a skater for Rose City, as Jessica Rodriguez in the opening roster, even though she uses her derby name in the digital program provided by the WFTDA (Figure 1.1).

Names became a bigger issue when, hours before roller derby was set to make its official live television return on ESPN2 in November 2017, players were informed that, "due to inappropriate material in programming" they would be bumped in favor of dodgeball and aired at a later date (WFTDA 2017). ESPN requested a number of name changes from skaters for the sake of FCC compliance. They targeted Frisky Biscuit, Beyond Thunderdame, Screw Barrymore, and Bicepsual. WFTDA complied by trimming the first of those three for broadcast, to Frisky, Beyond, and Barrymore. They fought and won to keep Bicepsual, on the argument that omission of the name would discriminate against a sexual minority. The board of directors voiced a sense of feminist victory: "After asking ESPN to do something it

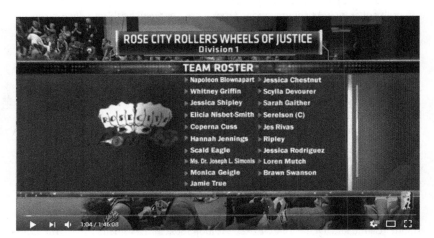

Figure 1.1 Screenshot of Rose City Rollers' team roster from ESPN3 broadcast.

has never done before, they are now prepared to run the entire broad-cast as-is. We believe this broadcast is a win for roller derby and the larger conversations about representation in athletics and corporate patriarchy."

The alteration of derby names undercuts feminist defiance. Aware of derby's history of co-optation, players put up some resistance to the professional, uniform model of men's televised sports, favoring to some extent their DIY protest and white feminist heritage. They deal with centrally-run mass media as a form of outreach to potential new recruits among women and girls, and have negotiated a contract that kept them in relative control albeit poorly paid. Roller derby is now positioned to expand space for women's DIY sports on TV, at the cost of becoming more uniform and monetized in ways that limit sexual deviance and the anti-capitalism of their riot grrrl origins. They play a larger bout against the neutralizing effect on rebellion of a centrally-run video medium.

Notes

1   As an example of this cycle, poorer people tend to tolerate higher demands from their more stringent religious groups, having less to lose from, and more to pro-test about, the world driven by wealth. A new and demanding sect at first draws such adherents. As congregations grow more bourgeois with mundane turnover in membership, in a regression toward the mean household income, they become less likely to tolerate the challenging preachers who warn against the sins of the rich. This pushes churches to become more secular or risk dissolution. Eventually, those who miss the stronger rebellion that growing churches have left behind must break off and form newer, stricter ones. The cycle goes on (Montgomery 1996: 82; Stark and Bainbridge 1985).

2   All names and identifying information of participants were changed to protect participants' identities and ensure confidentiality.

References

Bleyer, Jennifer. 2004. "Cut-and-Paste Revolution: Notes from the Girl Zine Explo-sion." Pp. 42–60 in *The Fire This Time: Young Activists and the New Feminism*, edited by V. Labaton and D. L. Martin. New York: Anchor.

Blinde, Elaine and Diane Taub. 1992. "Homophobia and Women's Sport: The Dis-empowerment of Athletes." *Sociological Focus* 25(2):151–66.

Coates, E., B. Clayton and B. Humberstone. 2010. "A Battle for Control: Exchanges of Power in the Subculture of Snowboarding." *Sport in Society* 13(7): 1082–101.

Cohen, Alex and Jennifer Barbee. 2010. *Down and Derby: The Insider's Guide to Roller Derby*. New York: Soft Skull Press.

Cooky, Cheryl, Michael A. Messner and Michela Musto. 2015. "'It's Dude Time!' a Quarter Century of Excluding Women's Sports in Televised News and Highlight Shows." *Communication & Sport* 3(3):261–87.

Edwards, Bob and Ugo Corte. 2010. "Commercialization and Lifestyle Sport: Lessons from 20 Years of Freestyle Bmx in 'Pro-Town, USA'." *Sport in Society* 13(7):1135–51.

Gieseler, Carly. 2014. "Derby Drag: Parodying Sexualities in the Sport of Roller Derby." *Sexualities* 17(5–6):758–76.

Harrison, Anthony Kwame. 2009. *Hip Hop Underground: The Integrity and Ethics of Racial Identification*. Philadelphia: Temple University Press.

Hebdige, Dick. 1979. *Subculture: The Meaning of Style*. London: Routledge.

Heino, Rebecca. 2000. "New Sports: What Is So Punk About Snowboarding?." *Journal of Sport & Social Issues* 24(2):176–91.

Kearney, Mary Celeste. 2011. "Tough Girls in a Rough Game: Televising the Unruly Female Athletes of Contemporary Roller Derby." *Feminist Media Studies* 11(3):283–301.

Kimmel, Michael. 1994. "Consuming Manhood: The Feminization of American Culture and the Recreation of the American Male Body, 1832–1920." *Michigan Quarterly Review* 33(1):7–36.

Loca, Chica. 2007. "Whip It-Marketing Session": Women's Flat Track Derby Association. Retrieved April 1, 2014 (https://wftda.org/wftda-whip-it-marketing-rollercon2009.pdf).

Lopes, Paul D. 1992. "Innovation and Diversity in the Popular Music Industry, 1969 to 1990." *American Sociological Review*:56–71.

Messner, Michael A. 2010. *Out of Play: Critical Essays on Gender and Sport*. New York: SUNY Press.

Montgomery, James D. 1996. "Dynamics of the Religious Economy." *Rationality and Society* 8(1):81–110.

Nguyen, Mimi Thi. 2012. "Riot Grrrl, Race, and Revival." *Women & Performance: A Journal of Feminist Theory* 22(2–3):173–96.

Pavlidis, Adele. 2012. "From Riot Grrrls to Roller Derby? Exploring the Relations between Gender, Music and Sport." *Leisure Studies* 31(2):165–76.

Riordan, Ellen. 2001. "Commodified Agents and Empowered Girls: Consuming and Producing Feminism." *Journal of Communication Inquiry* 25(3):279–97.

Sailors, Pam R, Sarah Teetzel and Charlene Weaving. 2012. "No Net Gain: A Critique of Media Representations of Women's Olympic Beach Volleyball." *Feminist Media Studies* 12(3):468–72.

Schilt, Kristen. 2003. "'A Little Too Ironic': The Appropriation and Packaging of Riot Grrrl Politics by Mainstream Female Musicians." *Popular Music & Society* 26(1):5–16.

Snap, Ginger. 2011. "Derby Names: Not Ready for Prime Time": *derbylife.com*. Retrieved April 1, 2014 (www.derbylife.com/2011/09/derby_names_not_ready_prime_time/).

Stark, Rodney and William Sims Bainbridge. 1985. *The Future of Religion: Secularization, Revival, and Cult Formation*. Berkeley: University of California Press.

Streeter, Rayanne. 2016. "Roller Derby as a Site of Resistance: Strategies for Countering Sexist and Homophobic Assumptions in Women's Sports." *Women in Sport and Physical Activity Journal* 24(2):143–51.

Strong, Catherine. 2011. "Grunge, Riot Grrrl and the Forgetting of Women in Popular Culture." *The Journal of Popular Culture* 44(2):398–416.

Thorpe, Holly and Belinda Wheaton. 2011. "Generation X Games', Action Sports and the Olympic Movement: Understanding the Cultural Politics of Incorporation." *Sociology* 45(5):830–47.

WFTDA. 2007. "Faqs": Women's Flat Track Derby Association. Retrieved April 1, 2014 (https://wftda.org/faq).

WFTDA. 2016. "Wftda Gender Statement": Women's Flat Track Derby Association. Retrieved November 15, 2016 (https://wftda.com/wftda-gender-statement/).

WFTDA. 2017. "Statement of the Wftda Board of Directors": Women's Flat Track Derby Association. Retrieved August, 2017 (https://wftda.org/news/statement-of-the-wftda-board-of-directors).

Wheaton, Belinda. 2010. "Introducing the Consumption and Representation of Lifestyle Sports." *Sport in Society* 13(7/8):1057–81.

2
FINANCING IN THE AGE OF MAJOR-STUDIO EXCLUSION

In 2015, Sean Baker shot a feature on the streets of Hollywood with iPhones. He had previously made television series such as *Greg the Bunny* (2005–06) as well as feature films. Still, he worked with smart phones (modified to capture high-quality images in widescreen) to stay within the budget limited by the absence of studio backing.

That lack of corporate sponsorship defines **independent** ("indie" for short) video production. As indies go, Baker's *Tangerine* was alternative in story and casting as well as in funding. It chronicled a day in the street life of transgender sex worker Sin-Dee (Kitana Kiki Rodriguez) and her best friend, club singer Alexandra (Mya Taylor). They make their ways across town to deal with a rival for a pimp's affection (Mickey O'Hagan), johns, bystanders, and hostile cis men (Figure 2.1). Baker cast this transgender story with non-actors from an LGBT community center.

After Taylor won Best Supporting Female at the Independent Spirit Awards, the largest competition for indies, the producers and activists who supported the video made Taylor and her co-star Rodriguez the first openly trans actresses to see Academy Awards campaigns launched in their honor. The project gathered much acclaim, though no Oscars.

This chapter explores how those with little corporate funding pull off feature production, and how opportunities have grown over the

Figure 2.1 Rodriguez, O'Hagan, and Taylor ride across Hollywood in *Tangerine*.

last decade to produce and market such video and to alter the look of gender on screen. From DIY movies shot with phones to large projects funded with venture capital, many groups must innovate to gain access to cameras and actors, much less channels of mainstream distribution. Online approaches to funding appear to have expanded opportunities, especially for female, feminist, and openly queer producers and stories.

The early film industry in the United States saw the reverse occur. Once photographers figured out how cheaply to record and project streams of still photos to make pictures move, filmmakers set up shops to capitalize on the new medium. They did this in ways that would close doors, rather than open them up. As early films became more popular and drew more audiences a century ago, the U.S. industry solidified in Los Angeles, and studios incorporated. Women had written about half of the scripts up to that point, but men who moved into the increasingly profitable and high-status business brought professional experience in crafts and trades, centralized control in a few major studios, and drafted contracts to channel profits into a smaller number of hands. As recorded sound came to accompany them, the moving pictures grew more lucrative, and white, male producers, directors, and writers took over the studios, pushing women out of well-paid creative positions and resisting competition by anyone outside of their own demographic (Balio 1993; Bielby and Bielby 1996:252; Koszarski 1990). During Hollywood's Golden Age of the 1930s–50s, fewer studios survived, and those that did centralized control over the industry. They used that control of production and distribution to write longer-term contracts for filmmakers and actors, which all but indentured many while advancing the celebrity of a few. Doors closed to anyone not tightly networked with the white men who ran the largest companies. Black filmmakers had to work in smaller companies of their own, with much less money to spend (Cripps 1993). Though white women remained important as movie stars in heterosexual tales of romance with white men, they could take few other roles or off-screen jobs. Hollywood became a guys' town and mostly told stories of white men's adventures.

This storytelling power has become even more concentrated in a few men's hands. Multinational conglomerates have since bought up the major studios that formed a century ago, leaving five majors that include Universal (owned by cable company Comcast), Disney (buying its venerable rival Twentieth Century Fox as we write), Warner Brothers (part of media conglomerate Time Warner), Paramount (owned by cable company Viacom), and Columbia (owned by the diversified electronics company Sony), which provide the capital for nearly all blockbusters coming out of Hollywood today. Alongside those high-capital behemoths operate several mini majors with smaller distribution networks, and then a raft of independent producers who scrape together modest budgets and depend upon the distribution networks of studios for wide cinema release. Majors tend to buy those "indies" once they make some money. For example, Disney has acquired smaller production houses Miramax (with Oscar winning films *Pulp Fiction*, *Shakespeare in Love*, and *Chicago*), Pixar (*Toy Story* and other animated movies), and Marvel (*Avengers* superhero movies), in addition to the television network ABC and, recently, its major rival Twentieth Century Fox.

These few major studios have governed much of the most popular video production worldwide, though they lose global importance as others around the world ramp up production and distribution. By maintaining such central control for so long, the Hollywood majors narrowed the gate through which excluded groups must fit to help shape gender on screen. They limit the roles that women could play in the most popular storytelling.

The Celluloid Ceiling Project, at the Center for the Study of Women in Television and Film at San Diego State University,[1] provides a yearly report of the number of women working in film and television. They found that, in the top 250 films of 2016, women occupied seventeen per cent of behind-the-camera roles including directing, writing, producing, editing, and cinematography; only seven per cent of directors were female, with proportions relatively unchanged for decades (Lauzen 2017). And, when men write or direct, the films are less likely to have female protagonists or to give women speaking roles. Studies of Hollywood production have shown that, when directors are members of excluded groups, their films are more likely to include characters that are as well (Smith, Choueiti, Scofield, and Pieper 2013). A century of industrial change appears to have cemented Western male domination of the industry and foreclosed stories that do not star them. For decades, even such white male independent feature-filmmakers as Baker were shut out, especially if they told stories that focused on marginal groups. Trans actresses of color, like Taylor and Rodriguez, went wholly unseen.

Within the last several years, two events in Hollywood have shown unusually bright lights on hidden business practices, by which studios maintain these forms of exclusion. Both led to calls for change.

Hacking Sony's Gaps in Pay

Both on-screen and off, women land fewer Hollywood jobs; and those few tend both to be white and make less money than the men do. Most such data remain hidden from public view, kept in confidence by studios shy about sharing their business models and the inequities built into them. However, emails released during the Sony hacking scandal of 2014 exposed large pay gaps between male and female actors and executives.[2]

Producers have long paid actors on the basis of previous compensation (the basis of each actor's "quote," with which agents begin negotiations) as well as their level of fame and the sizes of roles. They also divide compensation between up-front payment and back-end profits. The hack revealed that they do all of this in ways that leave women short. For instance, stars of the 2013 film *American Hustle*, actors Amy Adams and Jennifer Lawrence, earned seven points in back-end profits while their male co-stars earned nine points, despite the fact that Jennifer Lawrence was the biggest box office draw coming off of the 2012 hit *The Hunger Games* (Boot 2014).

The hack revealed gender wage gaps not only among actors but also among Sony's executives. Of the top seventeen employees earning over $1 million annually, Amy Pascal, the co-Chair of Sony, was the only woman; there were only two men of color (Roose 2014b). Columbia Pictures, housed within Sony Pictures, has male and female co-presidents, Michael De Luca and Hannah Minghella. The leaked emails revealed that, although both shared the same job title and responsibilities, De Luca enjoyed a base pay of $1.5 million and earned $2.4 million in 2014, whereas Minghella had a base pay of only $850 thousand and earned $1.6 million in 2014. She earned fifty per cent less than he did despite the fact that she had been employed by the studio for nine years longer than De Luca (Roose 2014a).

Actresses made public complaints after learning that they were paid less than their male co-stars. In 2016, *Shameless* (2011–) star Emmy Rossum revealed that she was paid less than her co-star William H. Macy. Though Macy has seniority in the industry, Rossum plays the lead in the show. After threatening to quit, and with Macy's support, Rossum gained a salary bump to match his and make up for the disparities of previous seasons. Like Rossum, *House of Cards'* (2013–) Robin Wright asked for a hike to match the salary of co-star Kevin Spacey, but was refused.

When the film *All the Money in the World* (2017) needed reshoots because star Spacey had been fired in the sex harassment scandals of the fall of 2017 (see below), Michelle Williams volunteered her time to rescue the film with reshoots. She was paid a minimal scale of about $1,000, while co-star Mark Wahlberg used his bargaining position to extract $1.5 million in fees (Mandell 2018). Unbeknownst to Williams, and despite being represented by the same agency, Wahlberg's contract did not require him to do reshoots, while hers did. As women's protests against endemic harassment grew (see below), Wahlberg's profit from the misfortune struck many as exploitive and as another example of the industry's vast inequality in pay. Under pressure once the disparity became public, Wahlberg later donated his fees to the sex harassment–victim legal fund in Williams' name. The agency that represented them both and permitted the inequity donated hundreds of thousands of dollars as well.

Leading actor Emma Stone has described the negotiations required for equity:

> In my career so far, I've needed my male co-stars to take a pay cut so that I may have parity with them. And that's something they do for me because they feel it's what's right and fair. That's something that's also not discussed, necessarily—that our getting equal pay is going to require people to selflessly say, "That's what's fair." If my male co-star, who has a higher quote than me but believes we are equal, takes a pay cut so that I can match him, that changes my quote in the future and changes my life.
>
> (Out.com Editors 2017)

The major studios have not gone out of their ways for such parity. Neither have they worked for racial justice. The hacked emails from Sony suggested an assumption likely to be shared by executives across the industry, that diversity in race, gender, and sexuality limits the interest of white and male audiences in the U.S., and turns off anti-black audiences worldwide.

For example, Will Smith ran into this racial barrier while promoting his early cop action movie *Bad Boys* in 1995. The longtime Hollywood practice of giving black actors prominent roles only in movies about struggles against prejudice in America had bolstered the impression that foreign markets were closed to black actors *per se*.

The Sony hack revealed the effects of such racial myths on casting decisions in leaked producers' emails that discussed the casting of black actor Denzel Washington and whether that would draw or alienate foreign audiences (Georgantopoulos 2014). Smith's action movies soon belied that impression, but it remains a Hollywood myth nonetheless (Yuen 2017:61).

In 2018, *The Hollywood Reporter* notes a persistent belief that "there's less of an audience for stories featuring people of color—that 'black projects' don't play overseas, and Asian- and other minority-led projects don't perform domestically" (Sun 2018). The reporter quotes an attorney for black personnel in Hollywood:

> If your analysis starts with, "We can't even fill out the line item for foreign," you are immediately discounted as not as valuable. . . . That myth has hurt a lot of product of color, and it's still a problem with the middle-aged buyers who are the proverbial gatekeepers, who in fact enforce that misperception by not buying content of color.

Filmmakers continue to excuse white-only movie casts in terms of returns on investments, in spite of careers such as Smith's, in ways that make racial disparities in pay even greater than those of gender (Sun 2018; see Chapter 5 on recent struggles against such whitewashing). These beliefs persist in spite of research showing that diversity in casting leads to increases in global profit (SSC WebTeam 2015:47–52).

Likewise, men who run major studios have long opined that films with important female characters do less well on the global market than male-centered movies do, even though analysis of box-office returns shows this not to be so (Hickey 2014). Comparison of male-centered features to those with female characters important enough to speak to each other about topics other than the male heroes shows that the latter make more money in the U.S. and at least as much money worldwide. The justifications offered for racial and gender exclusions are persistent, but probably endure more because of the privileges that they provide to the men who run the industry than because of actual financial returns.

Because these beliefs help to sustain exclusions, marginal groups remain less likely to gain high paying positions within studios—those offices with the power to advance and approve projects by and featuring diverse men and women. The Sony hack lifted the veil on studio inner workings, to show how executives shape casting and compensation with racism and sexism in mind, under the guise of merely giving consumers what they demand.

Telling on Men

Much of the inequality in Hollywood appears to result from exclusion from social networks, both from formal business meetings and from the informal party handshakes, jovial phone calls, and lunches at which people do so much business in this industry. To the extent that white men look upon each other and just a few exceptional women as the players to take seriously as parties to deals, most women still are seen only as currency exchanged among men, if they are not shut out altogether.

A surge of public accusations of sexual harassment and assault in late 2017 revealed that casting-couch exploitation of women as sexual currency still governs opportunities in Hollywood. *Quid pro quo* solicitations by men in a position to hire and promote women who indulge them combine with a steady stream of belittling hostility to make it difficult for women to enter the industry, or be taken seriously as peers even if they do find jobs. Under the pressure of such endemic harassment, Hollywood's labor market remains starkly gendered, treating women as arm candy, screen beauties, nurturing assistants, sexual playthings, objects of abuse, or outsiders instead.

The current wave of complaints began with a series of journalists' reports (Farrow 2017; Kantor and Abrams 2017; Kantor and Twohey 2017) of a decades-long pattern of sexual harassment and assault by Harvey Weinstein. He is the former owner of independent production houses Miramax and The Weinstein Company, which have made highly-regarded, Oscar-winning feature films for decades. The reports showed that Weinstein would invite young, female stars to private rooms, reassure skeptical targets that others would be present for talk of business, then corner them alone and try to draw them into sexual service, and demand later silence as a condition of advancing rather than harming their careers. As a well-financed producer, Weinstein could approve and fund projects, and shape reputations, on which aspiring careerists depended as they sought their next jobs and to join high status personal networks of the industry. This influence made his harassment a barrier to a group little seen in halls of power.

As an example of that capacity to make and break careers, popular film director Peter Jackson has confirmed that Weinstein spread derogatory rumors about actors who did not submit to his demands, such that they received fewer offers of roles and saw their careers dwindle (Redden 2017). Actor/director Salma Hayek tells of rebuffing Weinstein's bid for sex, later to find that he used his position as producer to sabotage filming and the release of her award-winning feature *Frida* (Hayek 2017). Weinstein could use women as currency rather than as business partners, driving them from the networks that determine success in the industry.

Accounts of sexual misconduct by comedian Louis C.K. likewise show that his harassment drove female peers to sacrifice opportunities for the sake of avoiding further abuse at his hands. Mentorship is vital to professional networking in the business of stand-up comedy; for female comedians seeking mentorship with men who take those opportunities to harass them, networking becomes prohibitively difficult (Belsky 2017).

We raise the matter of sex harassment in a book about gender in video because the practice both depends upon a set of inequalities that include gender and reinforces them. Those inequities render some makers of video vulnerable to exploitation by others, often driving them from the industry in a way that reduces the presence of women on screen. Many of the men widely accused are gatekeepers to video production. Andrew Kreisberg has run television superhero shows *Arrow* (2012–), *Supergirl* (2015–), and *The Flash* (2014–). Mark

Schwahn has been running shows such as *One Tree Hill* since 2003. Paul Haggis writes, produces, and sometimes directs successful feature films, such as two Oscar winners from 2004, *Million Dollar Baby* and *Crash*. Brett Ratner has produced and directed dozens of big-budget action movies, including the cop action *Rush Hour* cycle (1998–2007). Leading actors such as Dustin Hoffman, Kevin Spacey, and James Franco (also accused by multiple women or men) have produced in theater, television, and film for decades, in hiring-and-firing positions where they could silence complaints of unwanted attention and humiliations of younger women and men on their sets. Until a small number of women agreed to break the silence this year for journalists' stories, and by using their names, thus allowing rumors to turn into official investigations and draw other women to share their stories, cast and crewmembers felt little choice but to stifle complaints lest their careers end even more suddenly.

An unsung Hollywood screenwriter describes the exclusion and financial strain that both kept women from making accusations for so long, and keep women from advancing as fast as they otherwise would to positions where they could shape the stories on screen:

> Workplace sexual harassment predominantly comes down to job security and money. If you're paying women for their work, they're one step removed from complying with a harasser. Women made up just 13 percent of writers on the top 250 films of 2016 (the figure for directors was a paltry 7 percent), and when we do work, we're earning 68 cents for every guy's dollar.
>
> (McCarthy 2017)

This screenwriter recounts decades of stories of her informal networking and her dealings as writer-for-hire with male directors and producers. They ask her for such favors as under-the-table script doctoring for little pay and no credit. She took such low-reward jobs as investments, in the largely vain hope that the men for whom she toiled would repay her later with better work, on screenplays for which she would receive public credit and full pay. The hope for better jobs, and the informality of the networking that could boost her chances of landing them, keeps many women in a state of willingness to please men who ask them for favors, sexual and otherwise. Men use women for free labor with the vague promise of recommendations they may never provide.

For instance, actor Pam Grier worked for free on the script for *Coffy* (1973), at the request of the white men in control of the production, before knowing whether they would even give her the role (Quinn 2012:271) In this state of desperation, women become more vulnerable to sexual exploitation than they would otherwise be. Screenwriter McCarthy (2017) continues:

> If Hollywood is serious about ending sexual predation, it will have to begin by shaming people who benefit from free labor. . . . Money is the currency of a legitimate business. The accounting for sexual harassment and abuse begins with dignity and recognition in a credited job with a paycheck.

Hollywood's labor practices put women in compromising positions. Once there, they find that men so inclined will ask them for more personal favors, beyond free writing and under-the-table work. Many demand sexual subordination as well. Hollywood sends desperate women to exploitive men who can hire or fire them, and makes it hard for them to complain for fear of being cast out.

To the extent that many gatekeepers in Hollywood used the production system both to objectify women on screen to the amusement of male viewers and to subordinate women behind the scenes for their own benefit, they made the business a vast means of procurement, an industrial form of what feminist poet Adrienne Rich (1980) called "compulsory heterosexuality." They turn the industry into a way to drag women, including lesbians, into intimate relations with men as a condition of finding work.

One of the many actors to complain of harassment this year tells of producer/director Ratner going out of his way to humiliate her. Ellen Page recounts that, when she was eighteen and developing her own then-unannounced sexuality, Ratner toyed with Page in front of cast and crew by telling the actress who stood next to her to "fuck her to make her realize she's gay" (Fortin 2017). Luring, humiliating, or intimidating women into favors for hire, or at least for networking, and then threatening them with career damage should they complain, is how the industry impresses them into service. In that context, the inclusion of queer or transgender people in cinema, as in *Tangerine*, has proved even more difficult than that of straight cis women.

Both of these incidents, the Sony hack and the rush of accusations of sex harassment, have led to complaints and calls for change. Before we return to the funding of such queer cinema as *Tangerine*, we review the ways in which boys'-club networks of video industries resist the kinds of change proposed by women in Hollywood this year. Political pressure appears to be limited in its effect on exclusion.

Keeping Networks Closed

Studios have beaten back political calls for change before. Hollywood corporations began to hire black crewmembers in the mid-1960s, in response to Civil Rights–era pressure from the NAACP and the California State Employment Bureau (Raymond 2015:212). Their focus on race occurred prior to the rise of feminist and gay rights groups that would later push for other inclusions as well, but even that was too much for studios at the time. They lobbied the U.S. Congress against Justice Department lawsuits at the end of that decade, in a libertarian backlash by white men against affirmative action. By 1976, craft unions and studios had constrained racial integration to clerical and administrative jobs (Quinn 2012:490). Unions that controlled the best-paying and most elite jobs, in photography and sound recording, remained white and male. So did writer, director, and executive jobs in major studios.

These groups maintained their exclusions by sticking to informal hiring patterns not easy to govern or change: seniority rosters that limit the opportunities of newcomers, word-of-mouth rather than open-call job searches (Caldwell 2008:226; Quinn 2012:489), and secrecy about negotiations (Caldwell 2008:225; Siegel 2018), all without government auditing or enforcement (481). Those methods make it easy for executives to restrict pools of applicants, apprentices, and members to other white men, and to maintain salary disparities as well (Caldwell 2008:225–7). Due to the tight turnaround in the film industry, many jobs listings are not released publicly, and so networking remains the predominate means of hearing that new work has opened up. Exclusion from discussions in such networks of power prevents aspiring creators not only from developing experience and seniority and increasing their quotes, from learning their crafts, and from navigating the industry, but also from even hearing of potential jobs and what they should expect to be paid. The cumulative nature of reputation, and its dependence on a track record of previous work and pay, means that a little bit of exclusion early can have large consequences over the life of a career (Faulkner and Anderson 1987). Those dynamics concentrate white men in the Harvey Weinstein–type positions, where they can make and break careers on personal whims. As part of this concentration of power, industry contracts tend to feature clauses that protect producers' "exclusive creative prerogatives" in casting (Yuen 2017:13), safeguarding the personal discretion of the white men who control hiring in the name of creative freedom. As Yuen notes in her study of actors' battles with racism in Hollywood, producers there "use the protection of the First Amendment to bypass nondiscriminatory hiring laws" and thus reject whole groups from casting decisions on the basis of "freedom of speech" (12–13).

In their study of the gendered careers of Hollywood screenwriters, Bielby and Bielby (1992) note the consequences of the boys'-club structure of major studios, in which the personal discretion of executives, for the sake of the artistic freedom of their industry, reigns. Those wishing to break into the writing profession closed to women since the 1930s find that that employers hiring them

> are almost always white males. . . . With decisions being made in the context of high levels of ambiguity, risk, and uncertainty, social similarity is likely to have a significant impact on how

writers' reputations are evaluated. As a result, women writers are likely to remain peripheral to decision-makers' social networks and thus have limited access to well-placed producers and programmers.

(371)

Men in Hollywood have used the fact that, as a commenter on Hollywood marketing put it, "nobody knows anything" (Goldman 1983) to excuse their birds-of-a-feather hoarding of opportunities among those just like themselves. In this context,

> risk-adverse production executives in feature film might be more likely to imitate prior successful projects and to rely on rules of thumb that tend to typecast women writers. For example, no one wants to be the first to develop a script from a woman writer for a big-budget action-adventure film.
>
> (Bielby and Bielby 1996:249)

Because studios create movies with little knowledge of which will hit and which will miss and thus lose money, they can justify responding to the risks by playing conservative in their choices of people to hire and stories to tell. This informality of central control by the executives of few studios has kept closed the gates through which excluded groups must pass before they can alter what appears on screens. The men who govern that networking have been able to ride out waves of direct political pressure, as from the NAACP and State of California in these cases, and return to patterns of exclusion, of people and stories, in the name of artistic freedom.

Opening New Doors

Studios and unions do open opportunities for female, queer, and/ or nonwhite video-makers and stories when new technologies of recording and distribution and new markets promise new profits. We learned in the previous chapter how proliferation of cable channels enlarged the pool of stories that television could show, and how direct distribution from major labels to large record stores opened the music industry to gender and racial diversity as well, aiding the rise of hip-hop video and that of women in pop and rock. Both trends followed decades of closure and exclusion, of dominance by the culture of straight, white, professional-class men, a set of exclusions often justi-fied by the needs of free artistic speech and enterprise.

Business opportunities can allow for another type of expansion, as when governments alter interest rates and tax codes to make high-risk investments worthwhile. For instance, as he wrote and directed the black vampire movie that inspired images in *Daughters of the Dust* and *Lemonade*, Bill Gunn rode a wave of cheaply-financed, independent filmmaking that flooded the U.S. market in the early 1970s. Major Hollywood studios found themselves on the brink of collapse at the end of the 1960s, after years of expensive but unprofitable white fam-ily films. In 1971, they asked the U.S. government to provide tax shelters, to reduce the risk of spending and safeguard their profits (Cook 2000:11-13). In an unintended side effect, many small inves-tors far from Hollywood also grabbed the deal, sheltering monies in film production and hiring cheap talent to make the movies (Berliner 2010:199). This opened doors to filmmakers who had been shut out of unions and studios by the lobbying of that very era, as described above.

Results of this tax-sheltered spending included a string of black crime and horror films, dubbed "blaxploitation" for their bids to wring money out of black filmgoers with images of violence in black com-munities (Quinn 2012). Gunn's *Ganja and Hess* (1973), featuring its titular vampire lovers, was one of many, a movie celebrated among black filmmakers and recently remade by iconic writer/director Spike Lee (as *Da Sweet Blood of Jesus*, in 2014). Likewise, exploitation pro-ducer Jack Hill hired Pam Grier to help write and star in *Coffy* (1973), which became one of the most profitable blaxploitation films of the early 1970s and inspired black women across the country with Grier's image of vengeance on the men who poison her town with drugs and exploit her (Figure 2.2). When the government dismantled tax

Figure 2.2 Pam Grier as the vengeful hero, in a script that she co-wrote, in *Coffy* (1973).

shelters in 1976, and after a string of films that drew audiences too small to render the profits that studios sought, opportunities for black filmmakers largely dried up in the U.S.

Thereafter, until the next wave of opportunity (the 'hood movies of the early 1990s), chances for black artists to make movies in the U.S. in the 1980s were limited to franchise deals on studio terms for only the biggest stars (such as Eddie Murphy's contract with Paramount to star in three *Beverly Hills Cop* movies, noted in Chapter 4) and independent productions, most notably by Spike Lee (*She's Gotta Have It* and *School Daze* in the late 1980s) and Julie Dash.

As with the sudden rise of black movies in the early 1970s, LGBTQ videos such as *Tangerine* (2015) have done best outside the major-studio system. Independent makers of video have turned to crowdfunding for finance.

Crowdfunding campaigns solicit transfers of money online, in amounts large or small, to fund anything from charity to the production of feature films. While more charitable crowdfunding campaigns have gained prominence in the wakes of tragedies and disasters, such websites as Kickstarter or Indiegogo have allowed for crowdfunding of creative work. The earliest crowdfunding films saw theatrical releases in 2010 and began to increase in number by 2012. They include films unlike anything Hollywood majors have ever released.

For instance, Iranian-American filmmaker Lily Amirpour sought the freedom from studio control that tiny-budget filmmaking would allow her for *A Girl Walks Home Alone at Night* (2014). She raised over $56,000 with an Indigogo campaign,[3] abetted by a fundraising party in Los Angeles. Her access to an affluent and arts-oriented social network probably made this campaign more successful than it would otherwise have been. She has spoken of relying first on friends and family (Bernstein 2015), and research has found that initial portions of crowdfunding often come through personal connections (Agrawal, Catalini, and Goldfarb 2011; Mollick 2014). In any case, Amirpour wound up able to make a video her way. She produced a black and white, slow-moving but entrancing movie about a female vampire who terrorizes abusive men and little boys, with dialogue in Farsi. Feminists and many in the indie scene were impressed. Youth video–oriented production company Vice Media invested millions of dollars in her follow up, *The Bad Batch* (2016), with action-movie stars Jason Momoa and Keanu Reeves.

Like Amirpour, black and queer writer/director Justin Simien used Indiegogo to finance his 2014 film *Dear White People*. Its success led to an opportunity with the streaming site Netflix. Simien's co-producer Lena Waithe has also parlayed that success to a job as writer/actor on the Netflix series *Master of None* (2015–) and her new show *The Chi* (2018) on Showtime, giving voice to black lesbians.

Donors can choose among projects in a way that conveys a sense of democracy, where audiences come to feel as though the work remains insulated from conventional industry and thus remains authentic, perhaps representative of people otherwise excluded (Maule 2016; Ryan and Hughes 2006). They "attract those investors who are inspired by the desire to feel part of the production process of an audiovisual work and do not require additional return" (La Torre 2014:164). For example, when investors wanted to move the production of a documentary about the Flint, MI water crisis, which has victimized so many black families, out of Flint because of the lack of tax credits, filmmaker J.

J. Green turned to crowdfunding. Doing so helped him to guard the integrity of the film and give marginalized residents of Flint a voice.[4]

Likewise, funders seem to support those with whom they share a sense of exclusion, in the spirit of non-profit donors. Such patrons give in far smaller amounts than major studios do, which makes crowdfunding a tool for first-time filmmakers who seek niche audiences (La Torre 2014:164). Members of excluded groups can support each other this way, helping women who have been refused studio financing to complete their projects (Greenberg and Mollick 2016). In certain cases:

> Supporters are not only financially supporting a film, but also its cause. Thus crowdfunding and crowd investment schemes usually attract campaigning and issue-led film. The financial aspect is not the only benefit of crowd investment and crowdfunding schemes, and building a community plays a huge part both in promotion and the production and distribution processes.
>
> (Sørensen 2012:739)

Crowdfunding also allows producers to develop fan bases, for the purpose of marketing their work. Some view crowdfunding as "fan-ancing," as an exploitation of consumer interest for monetary gain and to pass the financial risks from highly capitalized corporations to people of limited means. Critics accused producers of the *Veronica Mars* film (2014) of fan-ancing, by passing the risk of an unsuccessful film from a studio that was hesitant to invest, to a large and active fan base that craved the follow up to the hit show (Scott 2014; Stanfill 2013).

With few opportunities for women and people of color in Hollywood, both in executive positions from which one can greenlight films and in roles that depict women, people of color, and LGBTQ people in ways that seem dignified to them, crowdfunding bypasses the traditional route of financing and opens opportunities. Much like indie studios are able to push topical boundaries that major studio executives feel unable to broach, crowdfunded films take more risks, creating films that can be seen as more politically driven.

In 2014, writer and director Gillian Robespierre released the film *Obvious Child*, using financing from the crowdfunding site Kickstarter. It tells with comedy the story of a woman who, after a one-night stand that results in an unintended pregnancy, seeks an abortion (Figure 2.3). While major studios shy from such stories in their appeals to mainstream audiences, independent studios and crowdfunding provide pathways for feminist filmmakers to stir controversy.

The queer romantic comedy *Boy Meets Girl* (2012) was produced on a budget not much bigger than *Tangerine*'s, funded partly by an Indiegogo campaign, far from Hollywood, in a growing trend of looking to web-video stars for (cheap) new talent (Yuen 2017:136). Like *Tangerine*, it also won a few awards at regional film festivals for its earnest portrayal of transgender life. The writer/director Schaeffer failed to find a suitable lead through talent agencies in the mainstream film industry, and found Michelle Hendley on her YouTube channel, where she had been sharing details of her transition on video.

Boy Meets Girl has been little seen and augured no immediate success for its lead actor. Moreover, it drew criticism for portraying its hero in isolation from other trans people, even though the character is obviously fluent in vlogging and would have regular access to a community online (Davey and Gage 2015).[5] That seclusion is key to

Figure 2.3 The hero of the feminist Kickstarter project *Obvious Child* trades a supportive smile with another woman who has received an abortion.

the movie's heterosexual happy ending, in which a moment of crisis directs the hero to the arms of her best childhood friend, an often insensitive, somewhat trans- and homophobic straight man (Figure 2.4). This rom-com resolution maintains a larger pattern in the genre, in which a straight man wins the love of his life without having to offer much respect or support. The film thus amounts to a political middle-ground, between the DIY video communities on the internet that have created space for trans perspectives (see Chapter 3), and the feature-film storytelling from the straight male perspective that continues to dominate Hollywood and all other major film industries worldwide (see Chapter 4).

For these two video industries to meet, a genderqueer feminist critic argues,

> it would take funding. Trans women are economically marginalized, and mostly lack the resources needed to launch artistic endeavors on the scale of a feature-length film with paid cast and crew.
>
> (Davey and Gage 2015)

Figure 2.4 The happy couple near the end of *Boy Meets Girl*.

Indeed, the growth of YouTube stardom (see the following chapter) has expanded opportunities for the overlapping groups of actors of color and transgender performers. Yuen (2017:136) concludes her analysis of internet and indie video with optimism:

> We are on the cusp of a new era of entertainment—one that can tip the racial balance toward greater equality. Not only have actors of color survived nearly a century of marginalization in mainstream Hollywood, but they are poised for a renaissance with the advent of new media.

The proliferation of indie cinema by means of cheap, crowdsourced production creates a market for actors and other artists who have otherwise had little chance to contribute to the production of video. It opens a door closed a century ago by the major studios' moves toward central control. The proliferation of crowdfunding is not the first breath of air given to groups long suffocated by the closure of professional circles in Hollywood. As we saw in Chapter 1, a cycle of renewal tends to bring capital and mass attention to vibrant local movements of excluded groups, who find themselves drawn at least briefly into mainstream video. These unpredictable shifts among industry patterns, based on new technologies creating new media, on innovations in tax and copyright law, etc., tend to lead to the largest openings for marginal groups. Such shifts appear to stand the best chance of reshaping the appearance of gender in video.

Notes

1   http://womenintvfilm.sdsu.edu/
2   An unprecedented attack on the computing systems of Sony Pictures, attributed variously to North Korea and to laid-off employees of the firm, disrupted most forms of business of the studio, including release of a film that mocked the North Korean government. The publication by hackers of email correspondence among executives embarrassed them by revealing their callous treatment of many artists in the industry, especially the many women whom, like other studios, they underpay. Sony Pictures Chair Amy Pascal, one of the most powerful women in Hollywood, was embarrassed as one of the writers of those emails and later quit, becoming an independent producer.

3   www.indiegogo.com/projects/a-girl-walks-home-alone-at-night-feature-film#/
4   www.indiegogo.com/projects/flint-6-film#/
5   This character type recurs among indie videos: a young, white trans woman who works a counter or desk and thus meets new people daily, who appears apart from any trans community and provides straight heroes opportunities to indulge novelty and broaden their horizons. For examples, see *The World's Fastest Indian* (2005), and Katie Holmes' single-mother drama *All We Had* (2016).

References

Agrawal, Ajay, Christian Catalini and Avi Goldfarb. 2011. "Friends, Family and the Flat World: The Geography of Crowdfunding." University of Toronto, Unpublished Working Paper.

Balio, Tino. 1993. *Grand Design: Hollywood as a Modern Business Enterprise, 1930–1939, Vol. 5.* Berkeley: University of California Press.

Belsky, Marcia. 2017. "The Lose-Lose Life of the Female Comedian": *New York Times*. Retrieved December, 2017 (www.nytimes.com/2017/11/11/opinion/women-comedy.html).

Berliner, Todd. 2010. *Hollywood Incoherent: Narration in Seventies Cinema.* Austin, TX: University of Texas Press.

Bernstein, Paula. 2015. "How They Funded It: 'A Girl Walks Home Alone at Night' Brings Iranian Vampire Tale to Life": *IndieWire.com*. Retrieved August, 2017 (www.indiewire.com/2015/01/how-they-funded-it-a-girl-walks-home-alone-at-night-brings-iranian-vampire-tale-to-life-66473/).

Bielby, William T. and Denise D. Bielby. 1992. "Cumulative Versus Continuous Disadvantage in an Unstructured Labor Market: Gender Differences in the Careers of Television Writers." *Work and Occupations* 19(4):366–86.

Bielby, Denise D. and William T. Bielby. 1996. "Women and Men in Film: Gender Inequality among Writers in a Culture Industry." *Gender & Society* 10(3):248–70.

Boot, William. 2014. "Exclusive: Sony Hack Reveals Jennifer Lawrence Is Paid Less Than Her Male Co-Stars": *The Daily Beast*. Retrieved August, 2017 (www.thedailybeast.com/exclusive-sony-hack-reveals-jennifer-lawrence-is-paid-less-than-her-male-co-stars).

Caldwell, John Thornton. 2008. *Production Culture: Industrial Reflexivity and Critical Practice in Film and Television.* Durham, NC: Duke University Press.

Cook, David A. 2000. *Lost Illusions: American Cinema in the Shadow of Watergate and Vietnam, 1970–1979.* New York: C. Scribner.

Cripps, Thomas. 1993. *Slow Fade to Black: The Negro in American Film, 1900–1942.* New York: Oxford University Press.

Davey and Gage. 2015. "Boy Meets Girl: Another Film That's Not for Us": *Feministing*. Retrieved August, 2017 (http://feministing.com/2015/06/18/boy-meets-girl-another-film-thats-not-for-us/).

Farrow, Ronan. 2017. "From Aggressive Overtures to Sexual Assault: Harvey Weinstein's Accusers Tell Their Stories": *The New Yorker*. Retrieved October, 2017 (www.newyorker.com/news/news-desk/from-aggressive-overtures-to-sexual-assault-harvey-weinsteins-accusers-tell-their-stories).

Faulkner, Robert R. and Andy B. Anderson. 1987. "Short-Term Projects and Emergent Careers: Evidence from Hollywood." *American Journal of Sociology* 92(4):879–909.

Fortin, Jacey. 2017. "Ellen Page Says Brett Ratner Made Comment Outing Her": *NYTimes.com: New York Times*. Retrieved November 11, 2017 (www.nytimes.com/2017/11/11/arts/ellen-page-brett-ratner.html).

Georgantopoulos, Mary Ann. 2014. "Sony Producer Says Black Actors Shouldn't Have Lead Roles Because International Audiences Are Racist": *BuzzFeed News*. Retrieved August, 2017 (www.buzzfeed.com/maryanngeorgantopoulos/sony-producer-says-world-is-racist).

Goldman, William. 1983. *Adventures in the Screen Trade*. New York: Warner Books.

Greenberg, Jason and Ethan Mollick. 2016. "Activist Choice Homophily and the Crowdfunding of Female Founders." *Administrative Science Quarterly* 62(2): 341–74.

Hayek, Salma. 2017. "Harvey Weinstein Is My Monster Too": *New York Times*. Retrieved December, 2017 (www.nytimes.com/interactive/2017/12/13/opinion/contributors/salma-hayek-harvey-weinstein.html).

Hickey, Walter. 2014. "The Dollar-and-Cents Case against Hollywood's Exclusion of Women": *FiveThirtyEight*. Retrieved August, 2017 (https://fivethirtyeight.com/features/the-dollar-and-cents-case-against-hollywoods-exclusion-of-women/).

Kantor, Jodi and Rachel Abrams. 2017. "Gwyneth Paltrow, Angelina Jolie and Others Say Weinstein Harassed Them": *The New York Times*. Retrieved October, 2017 (www.nytimes.com/2017/10/10/us/gwyneth-paltrow-angelina-jolie-harvey-weinstein.html).

Kantor, Jodi and Megan Twohey. 2017. *Harvey Weinstein Paid Off Sexual Harassment Accusers for Decades*. New York: New York Times. Retrieved October, 2017 (www.nytimes.com/2017/10/05/us/harvey-weinstein-harassment-allegations.html).

Koszarski, Richard. 1990. *An Evenings Entertainment: The Age of the Silent Feature Picture, 1915–1928*, Vol. 3. Berkeley: University of California.

La Torre, Mario. 2014. *The Economics of the Audiovisual Industry: Financing TV, Film and Web*. New York: Palgrave Macmillan.

Lauzen, Martha, M. 2017. *The Celluloid Ceiling: Behind-the-Scenes Employment of Women in the Top 100, 250, and 500 Films of 2016*. San Diego, CA: The Celluloid Ceiling. Retrieved November, 2017 (http://womenintvfilm.sdsu.edu/wp-content/uploads/2017/01/2016_Celluloid_Ceiling_Report.pdf).

Mandell, Andrea. 2018. "Exclusive: Wahlberg Got $1.5m for 'All the Money' Reshoot, Williams Paid Less Than $1,000": *USA Today*. Retrieved January, 2018 (www.usatoday.com/story/life/people/2018/01/09/exclusive-wahlberg-paid-1-5-m-all-money-reshoot-williams-got-less-than-1-000/1018351001/).

Maule, Rosanna. 2016. "Women Make Movies on the Web: Digital Platforms as Alternative Circuits." Pp. 23–57 in *Digital Platforms and Feminist Film Discourse*. New York: Springer.

McCarthy, E. C. 2017. "Perspective | How Hollywood Abuses Women—and Steals Our Work": *WashingtonPost.com*. Retrieved October 25, 2017 (www.washingtonpost.com/news/posteverything/wp/2017/10/25/how-hollywood-abuses-women-and-steals-our-work/).

Mollick, Ethan. 2014. "The Dynamics of Crowdfunding: An Exploratory Study." *Journal of Business Venturing* 29(1):1–16.

Out.com Editors. 2017. "Emma Stone, Andrea Riseborough & Billie Jean King on Tennis, Equality & the Battle of the Sexes": *Out.com*. Retrieved August, 2017 (www.out.com/out-exclusives/2017/7/06/emma-stone-andrea-riseborough-billie-jean-king-tennis-equality-battle-sexes).

Quinn, Eithne. 2012. "Closing Doors: Hollywood, Affirmative Action, and the Revitalization of Conservative Racial Politics." *Journal of American History* 99(2):466–91.

Raymond, Emilie. 2015. *Stars for Freedom: Hollywood, Black Celebrities, and the Civil Rights Movement*. Seattle: University of Washington Press.

Redden, Molly. 2017. "Peter Jackson: I Blacklisted Ashley Judd and Mira Sorvino under Pressure from Weinstein": *The Guardian*. Retrieved December, 2017 (www.theguardian.com/film/2017/dec/15/peter-jackson-harvey-weinstein-ashley-judd-mira-sorvino).

Rich, Adrienne. 1980. "Compulsory Heterosexuality and Lesbian Existence." *Signs* 5(4):631–60.

Roose, Kevin. 2014a, "Does a Powerful Sony Pictures Partnership Have a Gender Pay Gap?": *Splinter News*. Retrieved August, 2017 (https://splinternews.com/does-a-powerful-sony-pictures-partnership-have-a-1793844309).

Roose, Kevin. 2014b, "Hacked Documents Reveal a Hollywood Studio's Stunning Gender and Race Gap": *Splinter News*. Retrieved August, 2017 (https://splinternews.com/hacked-documents-reveal-a-hollywood-studios-stunning-ge-1793844312).

Ryan, John and Michael Hughes. 2006. "Breaking the Decision Chain: The Fate of Creativity in an Age of Self-Production." Pp. 239–53 in *Cybersounds: Essays on Virtual Music Culture*, edited by M. D. Ayers. New York: Peter Lang.

Scott, Suzanne. 2014. "The Moral Economy of Crowdfunding and the Transformative Capacity of Fan-Ancing." *New Media & Society* 17(2):167–82.

Siegel, Tatiana. 2018. "Sharing Salaries: How Actresses Are Fighting Hollywood's Gender Pay Disparity with Transparency": *The Hollywood Reporter*. Retrieved January, 2018 (www.hollywoodreporter.com/news/sharing-salaries-how-actresses-are-fighting-hollywoods-gender-pay-disparity-transparency-1075132).

Smith, Stacy L., Marc Choueiti, Elizabeth Scofield and Katherine Pieper. 2013. "Race/Ethnicity in 500 Popular Films: Is the Key to Diversifying Cinematic Content Held in the Hand of a Black Director?": *University of Southern California: Media Diversity & Social Change Initiative*. Retrieved August, 2017 (https://annenberg.usc.edu/sites/default/files/MDSCI_Race_Ethnicity_in_500_Popular_Films.pdf).

Sørensen, Inge Ejbye. 2012. "Crowdsourcing and Outsourcing: The Impact of Online Funding and Distribution on the Documentary Film Industry in the UK." *Media, Culture & Society* 34(6):726–43.

SSC Web Team. 2015. "New! 2015 Hollywood Diversity Report—Ralph J. Bunche Center for African American Studies": Bunche Center UCLA. Retrieved August, 2017 (http://bunchecenter.ucla.edu/2015/02/25/2015-hollywood-diversity-report/).

Stanfill, Mel. 2013. "The Veronica Mars Kickstarter, Fan-Ancing, and Austerity Logics." *Mel Stanfill*: www.melstanfill.com. Retrieved August, 2017 (www.melstanfill.com/the-veronica-mars-kickstarter-fan-ancing-and-austerity-logics/).

Sun, Rebecca. 2018. "Why Hollywood's Pay Gap for Women of Color Is Wider: Infrequent 'Golden Opportunities'": *The Hollywood Reporter*. Retrieved January, 2018   (www.hollywoodreporter.com/news/why-hollywoods-pay-gap-women-color-is-wider-infrequent-golden-opportunities-1075057).

Yuen, Nancy Wang. 2017. *Reel Inequality: Hollywood Actors and Racism*. New Brunswick, NJ: Rutgers University Press.

3

DIY VIDEO ON YOUTUBE

Hannah Hart uploaded her first video on March 16, 2011, "My Drunk Kitchen Ep 1: Butter Yo Shit." She shared it on YouTube for a friend, as remembrance of their days eating together, and never expected other browsers to watch. This recording of her downing a bottle of wine and trying to grill a cheese sandwich gained 500,000 views in three months. Hannah created more, in a series for her own YouTube channel. As her fame grew, she expanded to videos of advice, connecting more with her viewers. In 2012, she came out and now styles herself as an ordinary, relatable, young, gay urbanite. LGBT fans have written of feeling inspired by her example to come out to their families. In 2017, Hart posted new videos every Tuesday and Thursday to her YouTube channel MyHarto, which has 2.5 million subscribers and has given her an estimated worth of $2 million.

This experience is the epitome of DIY stardom online, where unknown creators become celebrities and conduits for advertising without having been selected for attention by producers or directors, or by having videos produced by them, merely on the basis of fan response to self-created content available for free. Where centrally controlled video industries reviewed in the previous chapter developed capital-intensive forms of production and vertical integration to raise entry costs and defeat upstart competition, YouTube videos remain relatively cheap and easy to produce, allowing for a DIY approach and thus becoming less centrally controlled and far more inclusive. This has broad consequences for the gendered content in the videos that appear there.

In 2018, YouTube has become a center of video culture. Production companies offer help to manage the celebrity of YouTubers such as Hart, teaching them to monetize their videos and sponsoring conventions where fans meet their idols. According to a PEW survey from 2013, over seventy per cent of adults online created or viewed videos (Moore 2011). YouTube's promotional version of its history dates the site to 2005 and claims over a billion users every day. According to *Forbes*, as of June 2015, some of the top-paid YouTubers grossed millions of dollars from the website (Berg 2015). YouTubers on this list create content that ranges in style from cooking shows and **vlogs** (video recordings of short, regularly updated, informal statements) to morning-show style chatter, comedy skits, and narration of video games.

How do YouTubers gain so much money and fame? The company created "YouTube Spaces" in Los Angeles, New York, London, Tokyo, Sao Paulo, and Berlin, where creators attend workshops to learn how to make videos. In the "YouTube Partnership Program," users learn how to profit from those videos, network with other creators, and use "YouTube Analytics" to follow their channels' growth and popularity. To be eligible for this program, YouTubers must draw at least 10,000 views to their channels. YouTubers who join gain revenue for each view, because advertisers sponsor the content and post ads to the webpages, and can offer paid subscriptions for viewers to watch content hidden by paywalls. YouTubers can also market their own merchandise and sell their products on third-party websites. YouTubers also often expand their enterprise to write books, tour with live shows, and create videos outside of YouTube, such as feature films.

In other words, YouTube is a corporate shell for DIY production, in which YouTubers create their own content but split profits with the corporation (Google, as of 2006) and expand commerce beyond the site. For instance, Hannah Hart has written two books, performs a live show for audiences across the country, stars in and produces movies off of YouTube, and has signed a deal with *The Food Network* to host a travel show. As an openly gay YouTuber, she has become a star of homonormativity, becoming for the internet what Ellen DeGeneres is to daytime television. She speaks of her hopes of becoming the face of lesbian romantic comedies on film (Keating 2016).

Popularity in the YouTube sphere is not without hostile response, however. When YouTubers' political statements conflict with those of viewers, tensions appear in the very same medium, as users post hostile comments, call for videos' removals, make their own videos in protest of those that give offense, send personal attacks by email, and even intimidate their opponents with shows of force at conventions. For instance, successful YouTuber PewDiePie claims that he meant only to offer commentary on what people in the twenty-first century would do for money when he paid two men $5 to hold up a sign that said "Death to All Jews." In his posted video, PewDiePie shows himself watching a video recording of two South Asian men who hold up that racist sign. His video shows him covering his mouth, appearing to be shocked. He received backlash from users and his sponsors for inciting anti-Semitism for entertainment. YouTube canceled their second series of his show *Scare PewDiePie*, and Disney removed him from the roster of co-producers of another project.

YouTube provides a medium for people to create and control their own videos. It does so in ways that differ from centrally controlled, highly capitalized production studios and their cinemas and cable channels. Creators can still amass profits in the millions of dollars from YouTube channels, but they can do so with far less facilitation by the captains of the mainstream industries. DIY culture is situated in a system where production companies still control much but not all of the space, and where some YouTubers more quickly rise to the top of the ladder while others remain on the bottom as a result of inequalities of race, gender, class, and ability. This chapter asks the following questions: How do marginalized groups use YouTube for both profit and activism? How are they treated in turn? How does the gendered content of DIY video change when production companies intrude and promise to help turn YouTubers into wealthy celebrities?

YouTube Culture

Though YouTube started as a user-generated content (UGC) website, professionally-generated content (PGC) has taken over (Kim 2012:58). These changes began when Google purchased YouTube in 2006, and monetized it along the consumer-capitalist lines of traditional media, such as television. After the purchase, YouTube started selling advertisement space on its pages and no longer permitted the use of copyrighted material in user-uploaded videos unless permission had been granted. While DIY, UGC still appears on the website, PGC has become more prominent, with corporate producers of video, such as the conglomerates who own the major Hollywood studios and television networks, using YouTube to gain profits through advertising online.

To the end of such corporate profits, YouTube compromises user control and favors the investments of highly capitalized advertisers by selling treatments such as "Promoted Video" and designating "Spotlight Videos" regardless of popularity (Wasko and Erickson 2009). YouTube features such videos on its homepage, drawing viewers (van Dijck 2009). Though users enjoy more discretion in a user-uploading site than they would in centrally controlled media, YouTube maintains control over what is most popular and easily available. Suggestions based on what users download, consumer ratings, and number of comments remain based on proprietary, secret algorithms, and structure what people can watch. Morreale (2014) makes clear that YouTube favors some users over others, especially with its creation of genres and algorithms that can recall certain users over others, and that creates problems for some YouTubers "in the YouTube attention economy" (118).

Still, YouTube remains a source of participatory culture (Chau 2010:67). In contrast to traditional media, the vlogging that appears on YouTube offers a sense of "authenticity" and community, as people communicate with one another almost directly, with little professional interference, in contrast to the cinema, broadcast, and cable videos more centrally controlled by corporate producers (Tolson 2010: 278, 286).

The divide between professional and amateur on YouTube is a spectrum, not a dichotomy. Burgess and Green show that PGC and UGC often merge in the contact between users who make videos and comment upon them, in a "continuum of cultural participation" on which people interact with the content (2009b:57). They see the "entrepreneurial vloggers" as muddying the distinction between professional companies and amateurs (2009a). YouTubers not only profit off their channels but also develop skills at creating content that people find entertaining and important, which helps them draw audiences to their channels and forge networks among fans and other YouTubers.

While YouTubers draw payment from the advertising on their channels, profits flow toward the privately held corporation, from the steady supply of largely unpaid labor that YouTubers provide as they produce content and build audiences for the advertisers that pay YouTube. For instance, fans of feature films are given license by the studios that own them to edit otherwise copyright-protected images and clips into fan tributes, which studios then deploy as viral advertising (Wasko and Erickson 2009:281). Fans become not only producers but also unpaid advertisers, from which marketing corporations gain.

Corporations that maintain these websites and other media can exploit the personal information and attention of consumers for profits, without paying DIY producers that actually draw viewers in very well, if at all. Advertisers profit from the social and economic value that YouTubers create with their online communities. Some YouTubers draw personal income from ads on their channels, but most do not, and the corporation controls all channels and profits from them all. While DIY production allows users who can afford video recorders/computers to circumvent the traditional barriers to media success, the website remains capitalist, profiting from consumerism and channeling most profits toward a relatively small group of owners. It is within this system, with its mixture of central control and DIY production of video that a small proportion of YouTubers rise to the top of the ladder and become small-scale stars.

Race and Gender in YouTube Micro-Celebrity

Theresa Senft coined the term **micro-celebrity** in her study of "cam-girls," who used still images, video, blogging, and crosslinking to present themselves as coherent, branded packages to their online fans. She defines it as the maintenance of an online presence "as if it were a branded good, with the expectation that others do the same" (2013:346). To maintain a following, a micro-celebrity shares personal, even intimate information on video and acknowledges viewers as her fans, to create a sense of personal connection (Marwick 2013). Unlike more centrally controlled star systems, where studios and publishers manage the images of their actors and pay reporters to limit potentially embarrassing revelations and maintain senses of mystery, fans of the micro-celebrities on YouTube idealize transparency and authenticity.

Not everyone enjoys equal chance to gain celebrity, because centrally controlled corporations continue to specify who profits from the systems under their ownership. YouTuber success is still based on profits from ads or being cast in studio television shows (Burgess and Green 2009b:23–4). Still, the relatively unmediated nature of YouTuber celebrity allows for some deviation from the corporate model, away from central control, such as Chris Crocker's popular "Leave Britney Alone!" video where he cries and defends Britney Spears. Through advertising and selling merchandise on third party websites, YouTube stars profit off of their brands with more say over their enterprise than stars in factory systems have enjoyed.

Micro-celebrity emphases on personal revelation and authenticity have driven YouTubers to share gendered experiences that more typically remain private, from those of harassment and coming out as gay, to transitioning genders. A popular YouTuber named JennaMarbles navigates the often-misogynist internet with parody as she plays with stereotypes (Wotanis and McMillan 2014:922). In her popular videos, "What Girls Do on the Internet" and "What Boys Do on the Internet," she exaggerates the performance of comparing her appearance to other women's bodies but also wanting to enjoy food and avoid hunger. She lampoons masculinity in parallel videos, drawing a beard on her face and masturbating to porn. She exaggerates gender to shed comic light on how we do it every day, and gains views while doing it.

Hard experience quickly taught many YouTubers that the gender and other inequalities that constrain life offline have much the same effects in cyberspace; early hopes of transcendence of categorical identity through avatars and anonymity quickly proved false (van Zoonen, Vis, and Mihelj 2011). For instance, the rapid proliferation of gender deviance and subversion works best for those groups with ready access to the tools of DIY production, which can costs hundreds or thousands of dollars. This is trivial in comparison to the millions of dollars required to compete for cinema screen space with the MPAA studios of Hollywood, but is still far above what many poor families can afford. Furthermore, groups redressing racist exclusion may be unable to draw much attention from the vast majority of users in North America and Europe, who remain indifferent, if not hostile, to their concerns. While YouTubers of color use the website to share perspectives on race rarely seen in centrally controlled media, the website is not as democratic as it might otherwise be, in part because the digital divide in access to tools needed to create content marginalizes poor communities (124), and in part because apolitical entertainment remains a more reliable draw for the viewings that generate much-needed income.

> A very important goal of these Asian/Asian-American YouTubers is to win hits for their videos. To achieve this, they must comply with YouTube's production logic, the logic that prefers entertainment to serious discussions of social issues, or what we call "LOL [i.e., laugh out loud] or Leave."
>
> (Guo and Lee 2013:402)

Gendered and racial dominance also owes to the confidence and sense of entitlement with which users assume control of the means at their disposal. Men have tended to use the internet as a medium more than women do, both as commenters and in uploading videos (Molyneaux, O'Donnell, Gibson and Singer 2008). Female vloggers were also more

likely to focus their videos on "personal rather than public, technological or entertainment subject matter" (10). And men have been more
persistent and vigorous in denouncing content that displeases them,
creating a culture of harassment and personal attacks that have driven
many women, especially feminists, off line. In a study comparing how
two popular male and female YouTubers are treated, scholars found
that the male YouTuber, Ryan Higa, received fewer derisively sexual
and violent comments than his female counterpart, JennaMarbles did
(Wotanis and McMillan 2014:920). Another study of portrayals of
intoxicated women on YouTube showed that, in sexualized videos
of women drinking, commenters were often violent and misogynistic (Rolando, Taddeo, and Beccaria 2016:8). The format holds much
potential as a public sphere in which people can exchange ideals on a
roughly level field of debate, but still conveys disproportionate hostility to women's participation (Szostak 2014).

Indeed, online harassment of women has become notorious on
the internet, with its decentralized and mediated structure foster-
ing anonymity and lack of accountability for disrespect. In a roundup
of research, Barak (2005:83) notes that "a harasser can take advantage of being unidentifiable, anonymous, and invisible, in addition to
having immediate, easy-to-execute, almost untraceable escape route
mechanisms," in a medium with a "(near) lack of clear legal boundaries, the absence of visible authorities and enforcement vehicles" and
finally "a culture that is characterized by dominant masculine values
and aggressive communications." In this context, women who post
feminist videos face constant risk and frequent incidence of being
targeted with threats, obscenity, and condescension, with results that
range from lowered self-esteem and heightened physical stress to
withdrawal from the medium (84). In some cases, however, recipi-
ents of harassment report wanting "to continue to engage in debate"
and feeling "motivated to do something" by the experiences of harassment (Lewis, Rowe & Wiper 2016:14). That resilience aside, the very
features of the internet that make it easy for marginalized groups to
network online make it just as easy for their persecutors to redouble
the pressure on them.

In addition to the challenges of gaining access, attention, and respectful support once online, surfers of YouTubers behold a wide array of stereotypical depictions. Guo and Harlow (2014) found that "the majority (64%) of the most popular videos about blacks, Latinos, and Asians included some kind of a racial stereotype, and the overwhelming majority (85%) of those reinforced or perpetuated racial stereotypes" (296). A study of drinking on YouTube videos found that images of women and men stuck close to stereotypes in other media, in which people take women's consumption of alcohol to signal sexual desire and loose morals (Rolando, Taddeo, and Beccaria 2016).

Indeed, the DIY space of YouTube offers room for people from all points on any political spectrum to air their views and affirm their senses of who they are and how groups look and behave.

YouTube in Activism

How are marginalized groups expanding community and challenging stereotypes through their uses of YouTube? Studies of social networking in the mass protests of the Arab Spring show that new internet technologies can connect disenfranchised people across national lines and share their thoughts abroad (Eltantawy and Wies 2011; Newsom and Lengel 2012). DIY culture matters more to groups marginalized from centrally controlled production and publication, as we saw among riot grrrls and skaters in Chapter 1 and independent filmmakers in Chapter 2; members of such groups have taken to YouTube to share subversive thoughts.

YouTubers contest dominant narratives of Muslim identity and sexual harassment, using vlogs to start discussions of social justice, telling stories that counter those of mainstream video. For example, Muslim women used YouTube to combat anti-Islamic hatred by creating video responses to an anti-Islamic movie. In 2008, Geert Wilders, a member of the Danish parliament, received intense online backlash for his an anti-Islamic film titled *Fitna* (van Zoonen, Vis, and Mihelj 2011). People took to YouTube to discuss the film in their videos and criticize its condemnation of Islam as misogynistic and terroristic. These authors examined how women responded to *Fitna*, and found that YouTube became a space for women to present their own images of themselves, which counteracted *Fitna*'s portrayal of them as either near violence or always at a religious place of worship, in traditional clothing and submission.

Queer people use humor to subvert sexuality and gender. The YouTube comedy channel *Spanish Queens* features queer youth who draw on LGBT stereotypes to challenge common views of them (Acevedo-Callejas 2016:142–3). Representing the cisgendered, white, middle class experience, these vloggers challenge both the conflation of gender and sexuality and popular visions of LGBT people as sexually dangerous (145, 147). For instance, a gay male YouTuber joked that his female friends always want him to do their makeup and expect him to give fashion tips (145–6). YouTuber Tigrillo confronts stereotypes of gay men as preying on heterosexual men by pointing out the absurdity that his heterosexual male friends must always worry that he will come onto them (147). Tigrillo jokes about straight men's fear of anal rape by referencing the large red dot on the Japanese flag (147). While *Spanish Queens* uses jokes to confront some stereotypes, YouTubers also tend both to affirm that men are overly sexual and denounce feminine gay men in their videos (149).

YouTube videos can subvert racial stereotypes as well, with alternative depictions of Native Americans. Kopacz and Lawton (2010) found, in their study of the heroes of such video, "that while he tends to be a man, just as in the mainstream media, he is our contemporary and not a figure of the past. He is a grown, civilized individual who is involved in community life, cares about the values of his culture and is not a violent savage or a militant. He is also less spatially confined than mainstream media characters" (14). For instance, in their sample, Native American characters were often the leads as opposed to background figures, and they were depicted stereotypically 25% of the time (10, 13). Native American video makers enjoy more opportunity to sustain their own narratives with UGC on YouTube because they can work directly with YouTube, i.e. their Partnership Program (14–15).

Furthermore, YouTubers can advance careers limited by racial casting patterns in Hollywood. With greater control over content, YouTubers of color can subvert stereotypes and post more extensive performances than the small roles available in mainstream video allow. As Yuen (2017:135–6) observes, YouTube stars are more popular than Hollywood celebrities among teenagers in the U.S., and may be able to sway casting directors with documentation of large numbers of subscribers that attest to their stardom.

YouTube is a space where people with disabilities can counter dominant storylines in which they merit celebration only to the extent that they cease to be disabled by returning to prior, "healthy" states. Against this normative "restitution" storyline, "Patients become the experts online in a massive power shift and people who never recover from their illness or who eventually die as a result receive as much agency as those fully realising the restitution narrative" (Ellis 2009:paragraph 27). Access to means of blogging and vlogging remains an issue, in a different way than it does for people with little money to spend on the infrastructure. Various disabled groups read captions and ALT text rather than listen to audio components of videos, for instance (Ellis 2010:21.8–9). Producers of YouTube videos highlight the disabilities created by refusals to provide access and the injustices that people thus disabled face, from exclusion in the designs of media and devices, to stereotypes that justify those exclusions. Their videos challenge viewers to rethink design and access and to stop settling for exclusions of large groups of potential contributors (21.4, 21.5, 21.9).

Vibrant LGBTQ communities on YouTube use the website to network and share their personal narratives, disclosing identities and experiences (Green, Bobrowicz, and Ang 2015). Wuest (2014) points to YouTube coming-out videos as giving visibility to closeted people in the queer community as well acculturating newcomers (26–7). People in search of guidance can both consume videos about being queer and create their own stories with relative ease (24–5).

As we show in Chapters 2 and 4, Hollywood film has mostly excluded intersex and trans people for decades, and then told a few of their stories in ways that rendered them as sick jokes, involuntary anomalies, or the vehicles of straight men's reform. To such depictions, DIY video offers an alternative, of transitions authored by people who know what they are doing and face daily struggles against the stereotypes on offer in mainstream film. On YouTube, trans vloggers upload their own narratives. Trans vloggers come out and reflect on their struggles, such as any uses of hormones and surgery that might be involved, or the responses they draw from others, and thereby control stories that were formerly told by unsympathetic corporations. These vloggers use YouTube to foster communities and frame transitions in very different ways:

> Trans vloggers become subjects, rather than mere objects, of representation, and often assume that viewers are young trans people like themselves. This collectivizing address is particularly powerful for young people who may not know anyone else who is trans.
>
> (Horak 2014:576)

Vlogs on gender transitions appeared in 2006 on YouTube, becoming popular and distinct enough to be considered a genre (Raun 2010). Transitioning vlogs are important not only because they give trans people control of their stories, but also because they contribute to activism, by challenging images of transgender people as passive and mentally ill. Vlogging allows trans men to assume the role of "expert" on their own experiences as opposed to medical professionals who have constructed what it means to be trans (Dame 2013:40). Some trans male vloggers act as experts in their vlogs by sharing knowledge and claiming shared responsibility to avoid enforcement of the gender binary. The public nature of these vlogs matters; they show trans bodies in a different light than traditional media do, such as in video diaries, where YouTubers show their bodies while on hormones or after surgery and do not treat their bodies as strange (Horak 2014:577; Raun 2012).

Research on trans men vlogs shows that their videos document their own history and visually share experiences of transitioning with others (Raun 2015a:704). Vlogs can help trans people understand their identity and often become resources for trans people to learn about others' experiences (Raun 2015b:8; Dame 2013:41). Vlogs connect trans people with others, bridging long distances for knowledge and emotional and economic support (Raun 2010:124–5).

Today, trans vloggers can do it "all online," transitioning and gaining knowledge and resources (Cavalcante 2016:109). This access, however, does not come without drawbacks. While vloggers can build community and find areas of the internet that act as "counterpublics," not all trans folk have access to these technologies; and outing oneself online can still be dangerous. The conventions of trans vlogs limit how people can see trans identity: "the talking head makes many aspects of social identity visible, sometimes reinstating existing social hierarchies" (Horak 2014:576). The celebrities among vloggers tend to be slim and attractive, the men muscular, most looking "all male" or "all female," and the most popular vlogger being white (576). These videos can also follow a normative pattern about what a trans man should look like post-transition and how they should internalize their understanding of their transition. Despite these limitations, vlogging helps "[t]rans youth creatively exploit the platform's predilections in order to author and affirm their bodies and selves, in the process generating far-flung communities of support" (573).

What about the F Word?

In the midst of such solidary challenges to inequality and revisions to gender, how do YouTubers discuss feminism? While more popular YouTubers who gain substantial income from advertiser sponsorship might avoid feminist controversies as spoilage of their brands, some YouTubers produce videos about intersectionality, sexuality, and gender identity, and explicitly label their content as feminist. They can partner with the website to monetize their videos. For instance, Kat Blaque is a trans woman of color and a YouTube partner who has 123,000 followers. She posts content on a range of topics including intersectionality, Black Lives Matter, trans bathroom bills, Ida B Wells, and critiques of Rachel Dolezal and transracialism. She has shared on her Facebook page that she has experienced so much racist, sexist, transphobic harassment that it's become normal to her.

Some feminist YouTubers have also crossed over into more mainstream entertainment outlets to reach even more audiences outside of YouTube. For instance, Chescaleigh is a woman of color and a YouTube partner who has 240,000 followers on her channel. She has also partnered with MTV to create *Decoded with Franchesca Ramsey*, a series of vlogs and comedy skits that focus on race and social justice. In its fourth season, *Decoded* features five-minute episodes on such topics as the connection between structural racism and voter ID laws, color-blind racism, and myths about Black Lives Matter.

The internet discourse is now sufficiently complex to feature debates among feminist vloggers, some driven partly by the click-hungry business model of YouTube. This system rewards vloggers for posting **response** videos, easy-to-make ripostes to other YouTubers' political statements. For instance, one of the most popular feminists on YouTube is Laci Green, a cis, white YouTube partner with 1.5 million followers. She partnered with MTV to create *Braless*, a feminist show featuring two to three minute videos about gendered products, slut shaming, gender neutral bathrooms, and rape survivors. When users search for "feminism" on YouTube, her "WHY I'M A . . . FEMINIST *gasp*" is one of the first videos listed that is not anti-feminist. In the spring of 2017, Green posted "Taking the Red Pill," proposing public debates with anti-feminists. This followed her denunciation of some feminist peers, whom she accused of censorship. In "Taking the Red Pill," Green calls herself "intersectional, sex-positive," and "questioning the seemingly unquestionable" by promoting conversations rather than trying to silence opponents. She questions the feminist idea of "speech as harm," in which permission of political speech exacerbates inequalities.

Feminist vloggers such as Kat Blaque have critiqued Green for ignoring marginalized voices in such discussions and for discounting the harassment they receive from antifeminists, especially from racist, transphobic YouTubers. She argues that feminists resist debates that merely validate racist, sexist, transphobic views as normal. Blaque explains that it is difficult for feminists to succeed on YouTube; that searches for "feminism" on the website yield more anti-feminist videos than feminist ones; that feminist YouTubers are often harassed and seldom achieve success; and that anti-feminism, by contrast, has become a lucrative business.

Given that feminism is not a popular topic on YouTube and often receives scorn from anti-feminists and libertarians, how do YouTubers discuss issues first named by feminists, such as sexual harassment?[1] Popular YouTubers have been accused of sexual harassment and abuse, and the ensuing debates provide a window on the place of feminism in online video.

YouTube abuse, wherein a YouTuber sexually abuses a fan (often underage) or colleague and/or sexually harasses women in public and uploads videos of that, dates back to 2012. In 2014, new allegations of sexual abuse surfaced for popular British YouTubers Tom Milson and Alex Day. Then, in September of 2014, Sam Pepper, a YouTuber who specialized in "pranking" videos, uploaded one in which he touched women's butts without their permission. Allegations of sexual assault soon followed. By 2016, such reports had inspired an outpouring of support for the victims, denunciations of the abuse, and calls for the banishment from YouTube of those accused. Laci Green and other YouTubers uploaded response videos renouncing Sam Pepper and calling for the removal of his videos from the site. These exchanges provided an opportunity to assess the degree of feminism overt in such online video dialogue.

Our content analysis of fifty-three YouTube videos, from March 2014 until February 2015, which responded to YouTube abuse, shows that only three explicitly denounced the behavior in terms of **feminism,** defined as recognizing that sexual harassment results from gender inequality and not merely from personal impulses. Most responses, fifty, framed the issue in a *postfeminist* manner, either as an individual problem, as a cultural issue unrelated to gender inequality, or as a result of an organizational power imbalance (between professional YouTuber and fan) that is also unrelated to gender inequality. Focus on gender relations among YouTubers in debate remains rare. For all of the politics informing YouTubers' DIY speech, video on the site deals in very little feminism, even in the case of a matter such as sexual harassment that only entered our language because feminists introduced it. The corporate-owned site has decentralized production enough both to lower its labor costs and give space to groups typically excluded, with the result of vibrant political discourses harder to find outside of social media. Still, feminism remains unusual, targeted with enough anonymous abuse from men that many women must avoid it.

As a DIY space, YouTube gives access to diverse groups of people to make videos and partner with the site to generate income, making the internet more inclusive by channeling attention and some money to groups long absent from most corporate mass production of video in the U.S. Nevertheless, group inequalities continue to affect people's chances of supporting themselves, much less climbing to the top of the YouTube ladder. Production companies structure the DIY culture by supporting YouTubers in different ways; this culture can perpetuate the earnings gaps typical of other industries: racial, gendered, ableist. Despite these challenges, YouTubers from marginalized groups have claimed some of the DIY space to monetize their content, build communities, create counternarratives, and spread feminist and other subversive messages. From trans communities using the website to subvert gender and share information about transitions, to feminists uploading videos in support of Black Lives Matter, social justice and counternarrative are alive and well on YouTube.

Note

1   Catherine MacKinnon was instrumental in drafting early legal approaches to sexual harassment of employed women, which informs sex harassment laws and policies to this day. See MacKinnon and Siegel (2004).

References

Acevedo-Callejas, Liliana. 2016. "Queens and Jesters of Youtube: Communicating Gay/Lesbian Identities through Humor in Youtube Channel Spanish Queens." *Sexuality & Culture* 20(1):140–52.

Barak, Azy. 2005. "Sexual Harassment on the Internet." *Social Science Computer Review* 23(1):77–92.

Berg, Madeline. 2015. "The World's Highest-Paid Youtube Stars 2015": *Forbes*. Retrieved July 10, 2016 (www.forbes.com/sites/maddieberg/2015/10/14/the-worlds-highest-paid-youtube-stars-2015/#4a2ec1773192).

Burgess, Jean E. and Joshua B. Green. 2009a. "The Entrepreneurial Vlogger: Participatory Culture Beyond the Professional-Amateur Divide." Pp. 89–107 in *The Youtube Reader*, edited by P. Snickars and P. Vonderau. Stockholm: Wallflower Press.

Burgess, Jean and Joshua Green. 2009b. *Youtube: Online Video and Participatory Culture*. Malden, MA: Polity Press.

Cavalcante, Andre. 2016. "'I Did It All Online:' Transgender Identity and the Management of Everyday Life." *Critical Studies in Media Communication* 33(1):109–22.

Chau, Clement. 2010. "Youtube as a Participatory Culture." *New Directions for Youth Development* 2010(128):65–74.

Dame, Avery. 2013. "'I'm Your Hero? Like Me?': The Role of 'Expert' in the Trans Male Vlog." *Journal of Language and Sexuality* 2(1):40–69.

Ellis, Katie. 2009. "A Quest through Chaos: My Narrative of Illness and Recovery." *Gender Forum* (26):1–12.

Ellis, Katie. 2010. "A Purposeful Rebuilding: Youtube, Representation, Accessibility and the Socio-Political Space of Disability." *Telecommunications Journal of Australia* 60(2):21.1–21.12.

Eltantawy, Nahed and Julie B Wiest. 2011. "The Arab Spring: Social Media in the Egyptian Revolution: Reconsidering Resource Mobilization Theory." *International Journal of Communication* 5:1207–24.

Green, Michael, Ania Bobrowicz and Chee Siang Ang. 2015. "The Lesbian, Gay, Bisexual and Transgender Community Online: Discussions of Bullying and Self-Disclosure in Youtube Videos." *Behaviour & Information Technology* 34(7):704–12.

Guo, Lei and Summer Harlow. 2014. "User-Generated Racism: An Analysis of Stereotypes of African Americans, Latinos, and Asians in Youtube Videos." *Howard Journal of Communications* 25(3):281–302.

Guo, Lei and Lorin Lee. 2013. "The Critique of Youtube-Based Vernacular Discourse: A Case Study of Youtube's Asian Community." *Critical Studies in Media Communication* 30(5):391–406.Horak, Laura. 2014. "Trans on Youtube: Intimacy, Visibility, Temporality." *TSQ: Transgender Studies Quarterly* 1(4):572–85.

Keating, Shannon. 2016. "Hannah Hart Might Be Youtube's First Crossover Queer Icon": *Buzzfeed.com*. Retrieved June 30, 2017 (www.buzzfeed.com/shannonkeating/hannah-hart-wants-to-bring-you-hope-joy-and-gay-rom-coms).

Kim, Jin. 2012. "The Institutionalization of Youtube: From User-Generated Content to Professionally Generated Content." *Media, Culture & Society* 34(1):53–67.

Kopacz, Maria and Bessie Lee Lawton. 2010. "The Youtube Indian: Portrayals of Native Americans on a Viral Video Site." *New Media & Society* 13(2):330–49.

Lewis, Ruth, Michael Rowe and Clare Wiper. 2016. "Online Abuse of Feminists as an Emerging Form of Violence against Women and Girls." *British Journal of Criminology*:prepublication online edition.

MacKinnon, Catharine A. and Reva B. Siegel, eds. 2004. *Directions in Sexual Harassment Law*. New Haven, CT: Yale University Press. (www.jstor.org/stable/j.ctt1npg6x).

Marwick, Alice E. 2013. *Status Update: Celebrity, Publicity, and Branding in the Social Media Age*. New Haven, CT: Yale University Press.

Molyneaux, Heather, Susan O'Donnell, Kerri Gibson and Janice Singer. 2008. "Exploring the Gender Divide on Youtube: An Analysis of the Creation and Reception of Vlogs." *American Communication Journal* 10(2):1–14.

Moore, Kathleen. 2011. "71% of Online Adults Now Use Video-Sharing Sites": *Pew Research Center*. Retrieved May 26, 2016 (www.pewinternet.org/2011/07/26/71-of-online-adults-now-use-video-sharing-sites/).

Morreale, Joanne. 2014. "From Homemade to Store Bought: Annoying Orange and the Professionalization of Youtube." *Journal of Consumer Culture* 14(1):113–28.

Newsom, Victoria A. and Lara Lengel. 2012. "Arab Women, Social Media, and the Arab Spring: Applying the Framework of Digital Reflexivity to Analyze Gender and Online Activism." *Journal of International Women's Studies* 13(5):31–45.

Raun, Tobias. 2010. "Screen-Births: Exploring the Transformative Potential in Trans Video Blogs on Youtube." *Graduate Journal of Social Science* 7(2):113–29.

Raun, Tobias. 2012. "Diy Therapy: Exploring Affective Self-Representations in Trans Video Blogs on Youtube." Pp. 165–80 in *Digital Cultures and the Politics of Emotion: Feelings, Affect and Technological Change*, edited by A. Karatzogianni and A. Kuntsman. London: Palgrave Macmillan.

Raun, Tobias. 2015a. "Archiving the Wonders of Testosterone Via Youtube." *TSQ: Transgender Studies Quarterly* 2(4):701–9.

Raun, Tobias. 2015b. "Video Blogging as a Vehicle of Transformation: Exploring the Intersection between Trans Identity and Information Technology." *International Journal of Cultural Studies* 18(3):365–78.

Rolando, S., G. Taddeo and F. Beccaria. 2016. "New Media and Old Stereotypes. Images and Discourses About Drunk Women and Men on Youtube." *Journal of Gender Studies* 25(5):492–506.

Senft, Theresa M. 2013. "Microcelebrity and the Branded Self." Pp. 346–54 in *A Companion to New Media Dynamics*: Wiley-Blackwell.

Szostak, Natasha. 2014. "Girls on Youtube: Gender Politics and the Potential for a Public Sphere." *The McMaster Journal of Communication* 10.

Tolson, Andrew. 2010. "A New Authenticity? Communicative Practices on Youtube." *Critical Discourse Studies* 7(4):277–89.

van Dijck, José. 2009. "Users Like You? Theorizing Agency in User-Generated Content." *Media, Culture & Society* 31(1):41–58.

van Zoonen, Liesbet, Farida Vis, and Sabina Mihelj. 2011. "Youtube Interactions between Agonism, Antagonism and Dialogue: Video Responses to the Anti-Islam Film Fitna." *New Media & Society* 13(8):1283–300.

Wasko, Janet and Mary Erickson. 2009. "The Political Economy of YouTube." Pp. 372–86 in *The Youtube Reader*, edited by P. Snickars and P. Vonderau. Stockholm: Wallflower Press.

Wotanis, Lindsey and Laurie McMillan. 2014. "Performing Gender on Youtube." *Feminist Media Studies* 14(6):912–28.

Wuest, Bryan. 2014. "Stories Like Mine: Coming out Videos and Queer Identities on Youtube." Pp. 19–33 in *Queer Youth and Media Cultures*, edited by C. Pullen. London: Palgrave Macmillan.

Yuen, Nancy Wang. 2017. *Reel Inequality: Hollywood Actors and Racism*. New Brunswick, NJ: Rutgers University Press.

4
PATTERNS ON MAINSTREAM SCREENS

Heroes and Beauties

The DIY video reviewed in the previous chapter arose in a context of mass production by corporations that employ business models decades old. Those of the global north have produced much fiction focused on straight, white, male heroes, who attain female objects of their desires by protecting them from other men. Groups who can portray the central players, young and beautiful white women as well as the male heroes and villains who chase them, take lots of roles on screen. Others find work in the industry hard to come by. This chapter reviews the history of this model and then shows how doors to opportunity open.

To simplify a rich history for the sake of deriving a pattern, we note that the film industry began with spectacle and trade in female flesh. Amidst their many images, nineteenth century viewing machines showed women disrobe and suggestively dance in "peep shows" for consumption by men (Alilunas 2016:45). An 1887 volume of illustrations of "animal locomotion," purportedly for science, showed women reveal and touch their bodies in ways that their male counterparts did not. Such gendered display owed to the fact that men ran cameras and directed performers (Williams 1989:45–6). They wanted women and could use film to collect their sexual displays. The stag films that soon developed showed stripteases and sex acts to arouse, screened in such venues as brothels or men's clubs, where patrons could bond over their trade in women's bodies (73–4). Traffic in women became both the topic and purpose of much early cinema.

Feature films lengthened to tell character-based stories, as audiences learned a language of motivated action that filmmakers could convey with images and few words. Movies shifted from the simplest spectacles and displays of dancing, shooting, riding, or even sneezing, to complex stories of many characters, made easy to follow by stating the goals of a protagonist or two. Actors became heroes, and sometimes stars, by portraying distinct characters with obvious aims, in stories of their attempts to meet goals (Bordwell, Staiger, and Thompson 1985:13).

The stories often focused on protagonists' aims of possessing women. Pornography of the day told of white women drawn into sex against their will but finding pleasure to their surprise (Williams 1989:50), just as feature films focused on heterosexual romance. Many stag films remained primitive for years, in the sense of leaving most sex unmotivated by any obvious character choices and desires; and much early film offered many groups diverse rolls to play. Still, Hollywood feature filmmakers shifted toward characters' desires as the drivers of longer, generic stories, many of white heroes drawing white women into romantic bonds, often by rescuing them from peril.[1]

This plotting developed in the context of race and gender relations at the dawn of narrative film. A century ago, Hollywood became the seat of feature production and industry regulation, through a cycle of alarmist films on women's sex work and "white slavery" that began with the release of *Traffic in Souls* (1913) and included Lois Weber's own *Shoes* (1916). Reformers feared what would become of white women who sought amusement or work in public (Lindsey 1996). The fall of U.S. slavery and challenges to imperialism in Asia had led Western powers to solidify constructions of race and idealize further the sexual purity of white womanhood (Arora 1995; Dyer 1997:127). Jim Crow segregation persisted, eugenic propagation of a pure white race was a matter of open debate among progressives, and the lynching of black men accused of assaults on white women was still well known (several dozen per year occurred during that decade) (Wood 2011). The racial importance of the sexual purity of Anglo-American women was overt and clear.

This vision of white women's purity solved a problem for filmmakers at the time, who ran afoul of censors for depicting vice and crime. Stag films displayed white women and their sexuality as prizes that male viewers could pay to glimpse in action. Mainstream filmmakers claimed higher moral high ground by putting such angels on screen as paragons (Dyer 1997). They also styled themselves as moral teachers, educating crowds about threats to the purest members of their society. In the "slavers" that hit cinema screens of the day, young white women who deboarded ships from Northern Europe and/or flirted in urban clubs were quickly swept into sexual service by brutal traffickers.

As Weber's career and the white-slavery cycle peaked, D.W. Griffith released his counterpart, *The Birth of a Nation* (1915), a celebration of the Ku Klux Klan's lynching of freed slaves whom they accused of attacking white women. In this epic, the prize is pure white, lit as glamour shots of actor Lillian Gish tended to be, as if she glowed from within (Dyer 1997:127) (Figure 4.1).[2] The sexual threat

Figure 4.1 Elsie (Lillian Gish) posed and spotlit as a delicate, spiritually glowing object of desire, both for the audience of the film and for the black villain shown looking at her in the previous shot, in *The Birth of a Nation* (1915).

is black, fittingly portrayed by white actors in blackface. The saviors are white men, led by the one who hopes to marry her. White women are objects of mutual desire: for villains, for heroes, and for viewers who enjoy their beauty on screen (Figure 4.2).

In an act of racial demagoguery echoed a century later, the U.S. president of the time made *The Birth of a Nation* the first film ever screened in the White House. He trumpeted it for what he claimed were its accuracy and its artistry, until later forced to back down after complaints from the National Association for the Advancement of Colored People (Stokes 2007). Though denounced by those they derided, such hit films set patterns in the plotting and casting of stories of race, sex, and gender that lasted for decades. Women on screen, mostly white, became sex objects pursued and claimed by men, whether victims, vamps, or both. They were lovers of male heroes and background figures, but far less often heroes themselves.

Figure 4.2 Ben looks upon his prize, bride-to-be Elsie, whom he has led the Klan to rescue from sexual threat, in *The Birth of a Nation*.

At this point, the film industry split. Studio racism left black film-makers without jobs and funding, such that some formed companies of their own, over the course of the 1910s (Cripps 1993). And, when the U.S. Supreme Court ruled in 1915 that the "business, pure and simple" of Hollywood merited no free-speech protection of its products, growing studios responded by promising to constrain the sex and violence on mainstream screens. Harassed by boards of censorship, they hoped to avoid regulation and loss of their public market (Sandler 2007:19). Pornography split from the white Hollywood industry and went underground, where it could avoid censors by remaining out of sight. Mainstream industry codes banned most allusions to sex from feature films, while pornography could pursue fantasies of men's possession of women out of the public eye.

In Hollywood films, young white women became movie stars, clothed but still coiffed and displayed as attractions for heroes and villains alike. An influential feminist theory describes this "active/passive heterosexual division of labour" in mainstream cinema. It serves as the basis of the typical Hollywood tale, one of heterosexual satisfaction for the white, male hero. Feature films gender their stories by making male heroes the driving forces, and white women the gorgeous objects they seek. This "split between spectacle and narrative supports the man's role as the active one of forwarding the story, making things happen" (Mulvey 1975:12). On screen, men make things happen by pursuing their desires. They want women.

Objectification of white women as the prizes men pursue spanned genres. Plots hinge on a hero's progress toward what he wants, often two goals per movie: a detective must solve the case and 'get the girl'; a soldier or spy defends his nation and gets the girl; a boy comes of age, defeats a bully, and gets the girl; a savior of a disaster movie rescues loved ones and gets the girl (Figure 4.3); a comic loser suffers humiliation but somehow gets the far-more-attractive girl.

In 1974, film critic Molly Haskell published *From Reverence to Rape*, reviewing a half century of screen images of women as evil or weak. She documents the turn toward punishing any objects of desire who resist control, as in 1946's *Notorious*. That film's heroes are

Figure 4.3 Jack overcomes death to get the girl, Rose, in *Titanic* (1997).

Figure 4.4 Viewers join the hero (at left) in an over-the-shoulder shot that aligns us in gazing upon the woman, whom men want. She will nearly lose her life to serve as object of mutual desire in *Notorious*.

a white heterosexual couple spying on Nazis as agents for the U.S. (Figure 4.4). Their assignment sends the woman to marry one of the villains, to her lover's dismay. Only as she lay dying of poison given by suspicious Nazis does he swallow his jealous rage long enough to come to her aid. An object exchanged among men at war, she finds herself doomed to a passivity that nearly costs her life. She will wind up tied to one of the men who claims her. The only question is which.

Horror films have pursued this possessive wrath more directly, showing what men do when any glitch in the system built to provide them women leaves them enraged instead. In countless television shows and movies, crazed killers hunt women and savage them until heroes step in.

The hit teen-horror movie *It* (2017) combines three of these plots: the coming-of-age story of a boy's defeat of bullies, the romantic comedy in which a loser gets the beautiful girl, and the horrific abuse of her by possessive men. A fourteen-year-old white girl, Bev, suffers molestation by her jealous father and harassment by local bullies while becoming the object of a crush by two of the film's young, white comic heroes, literally called "losers." One of the losers writes her an unsigned mash note, the other looks upon her with open desire (Figures 4.5 and 4.6).

In a comic moment early in the film, the crew of losers sun themselves after bathing, the boys united in a joint ogle of the semi-nude girl before them (Figure 4.7). Lust unites the loser boys, in a way that makes Bev an outsider.

Bev fights back against the town's monster "It," who seems to inspire the bullies' and her dad's assaults. That conflict escalates: Bev both starts and helps to win a rock fight with the bullies that results

Figure 4.5 The loser-hero gazes in awe upon the object of his desire, in *It* (2017).

Figure 4.6 Bev, the object of the loser's longing, as well as a victim of molestation by her father, revealed in the subsequent shot of *It*.

Figure 4.7 In a comic sight-gag in *It*, the squad of losers join in ogling Bev.

in a much-abused black boy joining their group; she then skewers It with a weapon, sending it into retreat; It incites both the bully to begin to kill and her dad to step up his assaults; Bev responds in kind, bashing her dad's head open. It kidnaps Bev at that point, putting her to sleep in its lair; the love-struck losers run to her aid. The oppressed black boy kills the bully, and the writer of the mash note revives Bev from her trance with a kiss (Figure 4.8).

The movie follows this boy's fantasy of kissing an unconscious girl with its romantic climax. Once the losers have vanquished the

Figure 4.8 In the climax of the movie, one of the losers saves catatonic Bev from It by reviving her with a kiss.

Figure 4.9 The final scene of *It* unites a loser and the object of his pursuit, in his forced kiss followed by her grateful response.

monster, the other love-struck boy overcomes his shyness to startle the (presumably recovering) Bev with an assertive kiss of his own. She responds first with a blank look, then with a smile, and finally with a kiss in return (Figure 4.9).[3]

The movie amounts to a contest among white boys and men for control of an object. Bev is strong and brave but, as in *Notorious*, rendered helpless and nearly killed by her status the as focus of joint desire. In the Hollywood ending, forced kisses from losers protect her from monsters. The girl in such a story will wind up giving in to one of the male characters who want her. The only question is which.

Figure 4.10 A cinematographer, as a member of the most male-dominated craft in Hollywood, signs his name to the gleeful objectification of women, in *The Fate of the Furious* (2017).

Today, as with the sex harassment described in Chapter 2, video industries maintain the procurement of young women as objects of male longing, traded as currency between filmmakers and consumers, just as they attract both villains and heroes. Video ranging from plotless stag films to prestige dramas makes spectacle of beautiful women and girls sought by men. Such imagery ranges from the carefully coiffed heroines of such high-status dramas as *Titanic*, to merrily outrageous T&A shots in action films (Figure 4.10), to the degradations of sexy young women in horror and porn.

In her study of the corporate organization of internet porn, Jennifer Johnson shows that producers profit most when women become objects not merely of desire but of abuse by possessive men. In the pyramid organization of the industry, content providers at the top contract with webmasters, who solicit payments from consumers of their video. They advertise with misogyny:

> Affiliate programs use the level of degradation and violence against women found in the content exclusive to that program as a marketing tool to attract webmasters. For example, PremiumCash.com markets itself as having the 'hardest content' (PremiumPass.com 2010) while Pimproll.com markets itself as

having 'lethal hardcore' (Pimproll.com 2010). . . . At IncredibleDollars.com, sites for promotion include HumanToiletBowls.com where women, with toilet bowls around their neck, are stamped 'degraded' (HumanToiletBowls.com 2010) just after the money shot or RockStarPimp.org where the webmaster is told that 'A glamour porn star model is destroyed' (RockStarPimp.org 2010).

(Johnson 2011:200)

At that far but massive end of video production, freed by the private nature of viewing from Hollywood regulation, makers of porn can dwell on the destruction of women that their objectification permits and jealous wrath inspires.[4]

Many performers in Hollywood have been able to avoid such treatment, either because they are so widely desired as A-list stars that they can choose among dignified roles, or because men reject them due to their race or age. Still, even the most well paid and widely admired young, white women suffer from this division of labor in Hollywood, losing most of the hero roles to men even if the few roles they take allow them their pride.

Other actors remain marginal to Hollywood cinema, because they face rejection. Old men appear as heroes mostly as male stars approach retirement age. Those men receive many such roles while, by contrast, old women receive few in Hollywood and mostly disappear. When old male stars take central roles, they tend to pair with much younger actors (Clint Eastwood and Al Pacino, for instance, have appeared on screen in sexual relationships with actresses as much as thirty-five years younger) (King 2010). Queer filmmakers and performers remained almost entirely closeted for most of a century, for fear of losing work (Russo 1987).

Race combines with age, sexuality, and gender to skew opportunities further. Smith, Choueiti, and Pieper (2017:2–4) surveyed feature films released in Hollywood during 2016 and found that over two roles in every three go to white actors, that one film in four had no black speaking characters, that one in two has no black women, and that three out of four gave no speaking roles to Latinas. As for the protagonists who drive the plots, two movies in three give all such leading roles to men. Of those with female protagonists, only three were women of color and only eight were over the age of forty-five that year (1). This litany of low numbers shows that the gender division, of narrative action from passive spectacle, remains in place and that exclusions have changed little in decades.

Sources of Change

As we learned in earlier chapters, opportunities to show films to large audiences narrowed a century ago, as white men consolidated distribution under a handful of studios. We mention here two related trends that have opened doors since: short-term increases in production, during which underemployed groups can find work; and formation of direct lines of distribution to niche audiences. We learned of the first in our review of the blaxploitation cycle of the early 1970s. We saw examples of the latter in our review of the televising of women's sports and the proliferation of DIY queer video on the internet. We recount the proliferation of niches in the television industry in Chapter 6, where we track the recent rise of feminist programming. Here, we note two other moments in Hollywood cinema history when doors opened because film cycles grew quicker and larger than usual.

The cop action cycle grew so fast at the end of the 1980s that producers looked beyond white male stars. In the wake of the massive successes of Eddie Murphy's *Beverly Hills Cop* movies by 1987, and the influential *Die Hard* in 1988, producers scrambled to make knock-offs. Some of them quickly hired such black actors as Denzel Washington and Wesley Snipes. Black heroism in cop action grew in frequency from one film in twelve to one film in four per year by the end of the 1980s. Washington starred in a string of such films, nearly one movie per year, until he won an Oscar for his role in *Training Day* (2001). A paragon of heroic manhood (Figure 4.11), he has continued to star in cop movies since, such as in *2 Guns* opposite Mark Wahlberg in 2013.

Figure 4.11 Denzel Washington was the most prominent black hero in cop action, here given the flattering hero-shot treatment in *The Siege* (1998).

In 1995, *Bad Boys* likewise made Will Smith a cinema star. He has since made franchises of both that cycle and the *Men in Black* films (1997–2012). In 2017, he co-stared in the cop action movie *Bright*, distributed by Netflix.

In a parallel experiment, producers tried a series of women, nearly all white, as stars of a variant, the serial-killer movie. Entries have featured such performers as Jamie Lee Curtis, best known at the time for early 1980s slasher movies. She starred in 1989's *Blue Steel*, which, like many cop movies featuring women, made themes of both the condescension that female cops endure on the job and the tendency of crazed men to pursue them. The most successful of these, *The Silence of the Lambs*, appeared in 1991 at cop action's peak, but the stream of variants included Angelina Jolie's turn with Washington in *The Bone Collector* in 1999. Though Eddie Murphy produced a blaxploitation-themed cop movie starring Angela Bassett in 1995 (*Vampire in Brooklyn*), the cycle has made very little room for black women.

Cop action has lost popularity as cycles tend to do after several years. It persists today most prominently as the twenty-first century *Fast and Furious* franchise, starring such men of color as Vin Diesel and Dwayne Johnson. The explosion of cop action in the late 1980s made a place for people usually shut out of such roles to become action heroes and major stars, though the intersecting disparities of race and gender remain and keep women of color to the sidelines.

White men continue to take the vast majority of savior/protector roles on screen. Their heroism rests on their capacities to defend innocents from harm. They were the heroes of hundreds of cop movies, brave soldiers in war films, and nearly all gun-slinging heroes of the massive western genre of the twentieth century.

Heroes of these genres run **protection rackets** based on the gender roles described above. A gender protection racket depends upon monopolizing violence, keeping women out of agencies of the law and bound to feminine standards of nonviolence, which in turn keeps women dependent upon men and willing to submit to them as girlfriends and wives (Peterson 1977). As in the stories of *The Birth of a Nation*, *Notorious*, and *It* reviewed above, women find themselves caught in the crossfire between competing boys and men who lay claim to them. The protection racket offers bonds with heroes as the only ways for women and girls to avoid capture and destruction by villains.

This separation of roles on screen was strict until the 1970s, with the occasional exception justified by a temporary absence of men, as in *Gone with the Wind* (1939). In that film about the U.S. Civil War, hero Scarlett and her sister-in-law shelter on their plantation while their men fight far away. Cornered by an invading enemy, Scarlett protects herself and her kin by shooting a would-be rapist in the face. The most watched movie in Hollywood history, *Gone with the Wind* echoed *The Birth of a Nation* by presenting the war that brought slavery to an end as a tragedy that left white women without good men to protect them from bad men. Later in the film, a black man, unmoored from the slavery that appears to keep blacks happy in that story-world, also assaults Scarlett; her male comrades feel compelled to lynch the offender in reprisal. Scarlett's earlier defense of herself stands out as an exception in Hollywood history.

This gendered character of popular video brings us to another moment when opportunity in Hollywood opened up for women. Costumed superhero movies drawn from comic books (e.g., *Blade*, *Superman*, *Batman*, *Spiderman*, *Hulk*, *Captain America*, etc.) became a fast-growing cycle over the course of the twenty-first century, in stories of male heroes saving not just threatened women but whole worlds. These movies at first kept most female heroes to the margins as supporting players in ensembles (e.g., the *X-Men*, *Fantastic Four*, *Iron Man* franchises). Carole Stabile assessed the situation in 2009:

> [A]lthough superheroes today are more ethnically and racially diverse than in the past, gender remains the third rail of superhero narratives. . . . Even genres that traffic in the fantastic cannot shake the mandate of protection: we can imagine that men can fly, but not that women can and should be able to protect themselves.
>
> (87, 90)

Women who did star in their own films of that decade stepped up to protection roles but still distinguished themselves from men by defending fewer and smaller dependents. Where such male heroes as Iron Man and Wolverine lead teams and prevent genocide to save whole nations or worlds, Catwoman (2004) and Elektra (2005) work alone, for personal revenge and to protect a child. This segregation of women by role in protection rackets has been standard screenwriting in action cinema for decades. As one writer reports of the trade,

> I know a male screenwriter who said he could think of 300 motivations for his male character, but all he could think about for his female character was that she had kids to go save. It's just a subconscious bias.
>
> (Galuppo 2017)

However, this gender gap in scope of duty and degree of superpower narrowed in the second decade of this century, as the cycle built upon the successes of early *Batman*, *X-Men*, and *Iron Man* installments. Where cop action fostered the careers of Will Smith, Denzel Washington, and Angelina Jolie by growing so quickly, major studios have now opened doors to diverse women.

Raven/Mystique of the recent *X-Men* movies (Jennifer Lawrence), and Natasha/Black Widow of the *Iron Man/Captain America/Avengers* movies (Scarlett Johansson) both play central roles in state-level protection rackets. They began in earlier entries to the series (*X-Men* 2000; *Iron Man 2* 2010) as sexually appealing, white supporting players. But in later movies (*X-Men: Days of Future Past* 2014; *Captain America: Winter Soldier* 2014; and *Captain America: Civil War* 2016), they challenge government corruption, lead teams, and make plot-driving decisions in contests over state power. When their earlier battles cost innocent lives and people demand better protection, these female superheroes remain central to the contest as protagonists rather than retreat or become helpless. They challenge authorities over their uses of military violence, and deploy those means of destruction themselves.

A movie such as *X-Men: Apocalypse* (2016) unspools like a military-morale film. Raven, disgusted by abuses of state power, has split off to work by herself and rescues fellow mutants without aid. But the movie hinges on her change of heart, as she gives up her loner status and heeds the call to duty in a unit at war. After Raven's pre-climax resolution ("Let's go to war"), she leads comrades to battle, barely survives the furious combat, and ends the film by training young soldiers to fight (Figure 4.12).

This undermining of men's protection rackets has only gone so far. To date, 2017's *Wonder Woman* offers the sole female superhero

Figure 4.12 Paired with the flight suit she will wear into battle to save the planet, Raven calls her comrades to war, in *X-Men: Apocalypse*.

to save the world as the lead of a film. Still, doors continue to open, as a few more black women enter the arena of combat in 2018 alongside the titular lead of *Black Panther*. Whatever the future of films in this cycle, women's movement to deploy state power deprives men of a monopoly on legitimate use of physical force and thus governance. Women cease to serve as objects of desire and become heroes who provide the protection. Such violence by women erodes masculinity and amounts to subversion of gender in video.

One could object to the use of women and girls as heroes in the most violent men's stories as white or Western male **fantasies**. Those in control of the industry cast performers from groups they exclude as heroes without otherwise altering the plots. The path followed by Jamie Lee Curtis, from slasher movies to cop action heroism, or by such characters as Mystique and Black Widow, from sexualized support to front-rank superheroism, suggests that female heroes of these film cycles may work at least as well as male fantasies than as feminist icons. And they may be white and Western as well, working as they do for a notoriously imperial government, in ways that cause mass death around the globe. The 2018 release of *Black Panther* adds a critical tone to what otherwise appears as faith across Hollywood superhero movies that the U.S. is decent and fair. Its valorization of a nation outside the U.S. is echoed only in the Chinese version of *Iron Man 3* not shown in the U.S., which features more cooperation between its hero and Chinese scientists and physicians than U.S. audiences saw (Kokas 2017:31–6). The Marvel superhero series has otherwise remained focused on the notion of basic American goodness as embodied by agents of the United States.

Likewise, women in pornography have performed for a century in scenarios written and directed by (mostly white) men, intended for men to consume, in an industry from which male producers make money on licensing and sales while most performers receive modest up-front fees, if they are paid at all. Though women began to create production companies for pornography in the early 1980s, and queer and feminist pornographies exist today, the massive genre that flourished with the rise of the internet continues to traffic in young women who control very little of it. Like the mainstream objectifications of Hollywood reviewed above, these videos trade in women's sexuality, in deals struck among men. The women on screen are mostly male fantasies, on center stage as "porn stars," but acting in stories written by and for men. Starring women in stories originally based in their subordination, such as protection rackets and the forced-kiss-satisfaction scenarios of early porn and recent horror, can amount to male fantasies if not rewritten by women in charge of production.

In a reverse of this relation, other changes to Hollywood plots may amount to **appropriation**. Where white or male fantasy casts excluded performers in stories crafted by those who exclude them, appropriations cast dominant performers in stories first authored by those they exclude. Groups appropriate when they star in and profit from stories and performances developed by those whom they have kept marginal. For example, cis or abled actors may star as trans or disabled characters, winning praise for what strikes critics as challenging embodiments. White actors may likewise star in stories that formerly centered on people of color (see controversy over these in Chapter 5). To explore the effects of industry organization on white/male fantasy and appropriation, we contrast different sources of video focused on the subversion of gender.

Transgender Imagery and Production Personnel

As part of the mid-2010s wave of feminist storytelling that we review in Chapter 6, consider Jill Soloway's television show *Transparent* (2014–). Popular video had long subjected transgender characters to prosecution for violence (e.g., episodes of *CSI: Crime Scene Investigation*) and constriction to work in the sex trade (e.g., episodes of *Law & Order: Special Victims Unit*). Transgender people violate the gendered terms of the protection racket by blurring the naturalized differences between the sexes, or at least by challenging medical sex assignment. As such, they have been left offscreen when not demonized or mocked. In an appropriation that amounted to a compromise with the status quo, Soloway followed then-standard procedure in Hollywood by hiring a cis male actor to play the title character in her series.

Nevertheless, Soloway also instituted what she calls "transfirmative action," by recruiting many transgender cast and crewmembers. Using the rapid-production, serial television format, Soloway can respond to current political contests with relatively little delay, and with her diverse crew can view gender transitions from many angles and focus on the stories of many women for many hours. A notorious episode lampoons a womyn's music festival for its trans-exclusionary policies and radical-feminist ambivalence toward gender reconstruction. Soloway has won much approval from transgender fans by doing so, appearing to tell stories that strike many as authentic and respectful, rather than as appropriations.

Moreover, Soloway hopes to alter hiring standards in corporate production:

> So I've kind of come to the conclusion that really the only thing to do—besides attempting to tell a full version of my story which includes confronting privilege, which is a white story, which are the stories we're telling for the "Transparent" characters this year—I also have come to the conclusion that really, my main focus needs to be identifying, hiring, teaching, grooming, distributing people of color, women of color, trans people, and giving them the space and freedom to tell their own story the same way [retail-internet giant/production company] Amazon has given me the freedom to tell my story.
>
> (Saraiya 2016)

Soloway has thus used the sponsorship of a large corporation to focus on diverse women and on telling stories of their inequities in their lives. By altering some hiring routines, she can address the organizational underpinning of fights over appropriation, the underemployment of the groups in whose stories privileged people star, from which video-dominant groups profit.

Such feminist approaches to queer stories remain rare, however. More often, trans people have gone unseen on television and been subject to appropriation in mainstream cinema as a fantastic plot device, urban exoticism, or the butt of jokes. In cinema, the rules of production differ from those of television. Projects develop for years, involving expenses usually far beyond the costs per hour of television programming. Major studios' feature films take months or years to write, more months to prepare, and more still to shoot and assemble. Any such film's release then costs millions of dollars beyond that, sometimes tens of millions for major event pictures, to market. The highly capitalized studios that produce such cinema invest conservatively, as we saw in Chapter 2. They hire white men in the vast majority of major roles: producers, directors, writers, craft department heads, and lead actors. White men encourage each other to "write what you know" (Yuen 2017:57–60) and treat dominant categories such as straight, white, male, and cisgender as the defaults for character types. Women rarely control that production, and nearly all queer personnel remain closeted.

The effect of this different production context has been to maintain twentieth century transphobic scenarios. If such men write about gender transition, they are likely to do so in ways that transgender people can barely recognize as authentic. Countless comedies (e.g., *The Hangover Part II* 2011) have appropriated images of trans women, mining quick scenes with them for humor, spurring moments of homosexual panic among the straight, cis male heroes. Others provide a sense of gritty authenticity to stories set in urban streets, where crews of streetwalking sex workers often include a trans woman or two. This small roster of roles to play has limited the careers of trans actors; as Trace Lysette explains in the PSA #ProudToBe, "we're not all serial killers and hookers" (Whitney 2017).

Lysette alludes to a long history in Hollywood where transgender characters, along with other members of the LGBTQ community, are often portrayed as sick, villainous, and sexually perverse. Hollywood shifted, from portraying its sexual threats as freed slaves, to making them queer, in the older sense of sick. *Psycho* (1960) notoriously diagnosed its feminine killer as a schizophrenic in drag. *The Silence of the Lambs* (1991) reveals one of its killers wants to skin women's corpses in hopes of stitching together a "woman suit" after being denied sex-reassignment surgery. Like many knock-offs that followed, that movie faced protests and backlash over that appropriation of queer and trans life when trans performers were banned from the screen (Phillips 1998). Still, the film would go on to win five Academy Awards and enough success to spur a decade's worth of serial-killer movies starring straight cis women as cop heroes and featuring sexual deviants as the monsters they hunt. Recent big-budget features focused on trans characters have included appropriations into sci-fi autogenesis (*Predestination* 2014) and hardboiled revenge (*The Assignment* 2016). Both depict medical management of sex-reassignment, but neither resemble the accounts of trans producers like those detailed in Chapter 3.

So it has gone in much mainstream video, in which filmmakers are mainly (at least publicly) straight and cis male, appropriating a few facts and myths about gender transitions to tell stories focused on the problems of (at least formerly) straight men. The antidote to that video diet will likely be the transfirmative action that floods production crews with people happy to subvert the gender ideals on which Hollywood storytelling was based.

Cool Black Women

In a reverse form of exclusion, performers long marginalized find themselves cast as gendered **white fantasies**. We finish this chapter by noting a small racial pattern in recent television, and the antidote to that white fantasy created by the inclusion of black and female creators in video.

The much lauded television show about the U.S. drug war, *The Wire* (2002–2008), featured among its second tier of leading roles a black lesbian cop, Kima. She is tough and uncompromising in a dangerous job, never shying from conflict. The show's creator reports that his "female characters are, to quote a famous criticism of Hemingway, men with tits. . . . Fictionally, Kima Greggs is based on a couple lesbian officers I knew, but largely, I write her as a man" (quoted in Lopez and Bucholtz 2017:13). The producer also notes that his team of writers, nearly all men, "largely ignored sex-based discrimination, feminism and gender issues" (Simon 2008). As a token woman in a fictional man's world that features no discussion of gender inequality, Kima fits into a white-male fantasy established in crime movies back in the 1970s: As gay and black, she is skillful, courageous, morally scrupulous, and mostly marginal to the plot. Little based on actual women, she is free of complexity and has no character arc on which the show's storyline would focus. She is a changeless paragon of beauty, strength, and virtue. She is a **Cool Black Woman** (CBW) in progressive, white storytelling.

The CBW is notable but not central, important in her accomplishments but not the star whose changes of heart drive the story. She moves heroes around their obstacles by courage and skill that those white characters cannot match; but her personal struggles are never in focus, and she has very little to do with other main black characters. She is a plot function in service of white protagonism. We write *protagonism*, not heroism, because a CBW is *heroic* in the limited sense of combining strength and insight with virtue. She sees what must be done and makes it happen. But she is not a principal protagonist, not the star.

Manatu (2003:204) notes the "all-knowing" seers who guide white men through their journeys in such films as *The Matrix*, modern versions of the reliable mammies of early cinema. CBWs on feminist television include the loyal partner of the white trans woman in *Sense8* (2015–2017), who supports and even rescues the white star but who has no story of her own. *The Handmaid's Tale* (2017) is likewise focused on a white protagonist of a feminist story, one imprisoned in a patrimonial police state, and whose black friend manages to escape her bondage twice, the second time dispatching letters of solidarity to buoy the protagonist.

The yoga instructor of the award-winning feminist series *Big Little Lies* (2017) is the ideal woman in her community, remaining above the backbiting fray in which the four white principals flounder (Figure 4.13). She saves the victims among them with her decisive move against an aggravated rapist. Because the story, set in a wealthy California coastal community, features people of color mainly as background figures in contexts of performance (the CBW's yoga class, the band at a community concert), her minority status stands out. At the end of the show's first season, five women and their children lounge on a beach, having found solidarity in their struggle against gendered violence. However, one divide persists, not on the beach but in the storytelling. The four white women have been protagonists in extended storylines, all told with tight close-ups on pained expressions to highlight their inner lives. The CBW, by contrast, has less personal history with the others and has never been focus of a story of her own. She has been an outsider to the group and marginal to the series.

The CBW in each of these stories disappears for much of the running time and appears when in contact with or in aid of the white protagonists (or, in the case of *Big Little Lies*, with their male partners,

Figure 4.13 The Cool Black Woman looks skeptically upon a hapless white man in *Big Little Lies*.

to talk about the white women). None of these stories would pass a racial Bechdel test.[5] Her appearance in a string of progressive television shows, and concentration in the feminist ones, suggests that she incarnates a white, leftist impulse to acknowledge and laud black women without focusing on them for very long.

White fantasy is the use of people of color in stories based on white life, accomplished in part by keeping actors of color hungry for work, likely to take and even be grateful for projects that might otherwise strike them as limiting.

We suggest that people, given fair access to means of production, need fear no such exploitation. They can present themselves as they wish, both as heroes and in stories that honor their experiences. But black women were driven from mainstream screens a century ago, featured in Hollywood movies for decades mainly as maids and other figures of support to whites who star as objects of desire, and then, with the rise of blaxploitation, also as oversexed molls in tales of urban crime (Manatu 2003). To the extent that second-wave feminism combined with the Civil Rights movement to make black women cool without giving them steady work in pop-video production, it tends to limit them to white and male fantasies when not ignoring them altogether. Filmmakers such as Julie Dash have trouble seeing their projects made. Only in the twenty-first century have such producers as Tyler Perry, Shonda Rhimes, and Ava DuVernay helped to place black women in a critical mass of starring roles, in stories written by or at least for black women. In this context, a raunchy comedy such as *Girls Trip* (2017) means more than it otherwise would.

Girls Trip, based on stories by black female screenwriters and otherwise written, produced, and directed by black men, works as a follow-up to the famous 1995 celebration of sisterhood, *Waiting to Exhale*. That plot (based on black female screenwriter Terry McMillan's book, as directed by a black man) hinged on four black women's progress through romantic relationships with men, including that of a television producer played by Whitney Houston. The film ends when most of the four heroes give up on men and affirm their friendships instead. Springer (2007:269) locates the film in a series of postfeminist retreats on the part of black female heroes, who turn from misfortunes at the hands of wealthy men, urban life, or ritzy white employers, back to black communities and especially to circles of black female friends. Such retreats amount to "coming back to blackness—the implication being that when a black female protagonist has it all she becomes a snob and is in danger of no longer being authentically black" (272). *Girls Trip* provides a version of this, separating its four straight heroes from men via divorce and other conflict, ending on a note of sisterly solidarity in the celebration of black bourgeois life at the Essence Festival (see Introduction and Figure 4.14).

In the main plot of *Girls Trip*, television lifestyle-advisor Ryan rejects her cohost/husband over his infidelity and the threat that it poses to her self-confidence and career. Her dramatic arc begins with denial in hopes of maintaining the telegenic illusion of marital bliss. Over the course of the story, Ryan's "posse" of three longtime friends encourage her to see how precarious her position has become, depending as she does on a faithless man. Along the way, the film mocks her delusions of control over the situation: "If I will it, I *can* have it all" she chants on television, to no avail. Ryan's friends encourage her to seek divorce; and, at the crisis point, Ryan rejects them in favor of her husband (Figure 4.14).

Figure 4.14 Ryan at the crisis point on her character arc, having rejected her friends, in *Girls Trip*. The hero's close-up emphasizes her deliberation and beauty without making her the object of a man's gaze.

The film ends with a cliché from romantic comedy, as her friends race across town to repair the severed bond. Inspired by the sight, Ryan reverses herself one last time to embrace them over her man. As strictly heterosexual as *Girls Trip* is, the reconciliation is sororal. Ryan praises "my girls" for reminding her of "a time when I didn't fear anything." She preaches that "No one has the power to shatter your dreams unless you give it to them." In the conclusion, Ryan and one of her friends accept corporate funding for a new television show. This blend of sisterhood and individualism amounts to a middle ground between feminism and the more common post feminism of Hollywood. These girls get each other.

Girls Trip avoids the gendered white fantasy of the Cool Black Woman that we find in feminist television. Instead, it brings black women up front and center, giving Ryan a hero's close-ups and dramatic arc, as well as a posse of sisters who support her. A century after black women were mostly driven from center screen to become background figures, and black filmmakers had to form separate production companies doomed to fail in competition with the better-funded majors, the exceptional nature of this hit suggests the extent of the ground to be won. It indicates the importance of increased inclusion of black women and men as producers of popular video. Like *Waiting to Exhale* before it, this hit may leave audiences unsatisfied if they look for a more diverse set of black women on screen. Only in the context of lots of production by black women and men, of many different kinds of stories, are movies such as this likely to leave most everyone satisfied.

In that sense, *Girls Trip* joins a relatively small group of films "deliberately conceived as a film about black women, with black women intended as its primary audience," as Jacqueline Bobo wrote of *Daughters of the Dust* (1995:165). That film, she continues, "intervenes strongly in a tradition of derogatory portrayals of black women in dominant cinema."

Opportunities for such intervention have been opening for black artists, in the wake of the success of Shonda Rhimes in television and years of mid-level success of inexpensive black comedies in cinema. In 2014, the venerable network ABC dedicated an entire (Thursday) night, playfully dubbed TGIT, of programming to Rhimes' shows, including *Grey's Anatomy* (2005–), *Scandal* (2012–), *How to Get Away With Murder* (2014–), and *The Catch* (2016–2017). Donald Glover became a critic favorite with *Atlanta* (2016–), focused on that city's rap scene and winning Golden Globes in 2017. He made headlines for his decision to employ all black writers in an effort to "show white people, 'you don't know everything about black culture'" (Browne 2016). And *Girls Trip* has also provided another in a string of successes for the black male director Malcolm Lee. Trained on Spike Lee movie sets during the 1990s, Lee has directed minor-hit comedies every few years since *Best Man* (1999).

The rapid expansion of superhero cycles, a century after the scandals over *The Birth of a Nation*, brings a cast of black heroes to what Maryann Erigha (2016) shows has otherwise been white-authored cinema. *Black Panther* (2018), written and directed by black men, has inspired at least some among its fans regard it as having sidestepped white fantasy and appropriation, as they plan to see it with all-black audiences:

> We'll be able to take the mask off. . . . It's going to be really subtle, but we're going to get certain things about the movie and its language that only we know. So I want this to be something we do together: my family, my chapter and my community.
>
> (quoted in Tillet 2018)

Makers of video have slipped old race and gender constraints under a few conditions: rewrites of women's roles in attempts to draw female viewers; rapid growth of film and television cycles that allow excluded groups to take hero roles; and the opening for more political storytelling presented by niche-marketed, rapid-production television. Such trends appear to have combined to loosen constraints on appearances of black women in popular video, though not without decades of difficult struggle. Accepting an award for her performance as one of the posse in *Girls Trip* from the New York Film Critics Circle in January 2018, middle-aged actress Tiffany Haddish spoke of inclusion in the star factory of popular video:

> I'm glad you see me, because it's been so many years nobody saw me. When you're a little kid going through the [foster-care] system, you wonder, "Does anybody even know I'm alive?" To be able to be this example to so many youth. . . . There's so many people like me that you guys have no clue about. But they're coming, because I kicked the fucking door open.

Notes

1   We simplify whiteness for the purposes of making a clear point about race. But Diana Negra (2001) has shown that ethnic options within whiteness complicated the sexual innocence of many white stars, adding touches of "unauthorized sexuality" (18) in some cases, and providing a form of character difference alternative to the more sensitive ones of race or class (17).

2   Dyer's point is that cinematographers and portrait artists often both spotlit and backlit white women to suggest an inner, spiritual glow, one strong enough to illuminate the white man who claims her as well (1997:127–40).

3   In the Stephen King novel on which this movie was based, all of the male losers cement their bonds by having sex with Beverly after they defeat It.

4   As we show in Chapter Five, these presentations of white women as objects of men's pursuit could lead to national scandal, as Arora (1995) shows in her history of British debate over Hollywood depictions of brown-skin sexual threats "imperilling the prestige of the white woman" in Colonial India of the 1920s.

5   Hickey, Koeze, Dottle, and Wezerek (2017) invented variations on the Bechdel test, which in its original form judged a movie by three criteria: It has to have at least two women in it, who talk to each other, about something beside a man (Bechdel 1986:22–3). Their variations include tests for the presence of women and men of color before and behind the cameras and the interactions between such characters on screen.

References

Alilunas, Peter. 2016. *Smutty Little Movies: The Creation and Regulation of Adult Video*. Berkeley: University of California Press.

Arora, Poonam. 1995. "'Imperilling the Prestige of the White Woman': Colonial Anxiety and Film Censorship in British India." *Visual Anthropology Review* 11(2):36–50.

Bechdel, Alison. 1986. *Dykes to Watch Out For*. Ithaca, NY: Firebrand Books.

Bobo, Jacqueline. 1995. *Black Women as Cultural Readers*. New York: Columbia University Press.

Bordwell, David, Janet Staiger and Kristin Thompson. 1985. *The Classical Hollywood Cinema: Film Style and Mode of Production to 1960*. New York: Columbia University Press.

Browne, Rembert. 2016. "Donald Glover Turns His Eye to His Hometown—and Black America—in Atlanta": *vulture.com*. Retrieved August, 2017 (www.vulture.com/2016/08/donald-glover-atlanta.html).

Cripps, Thomas. 1993. *Slow Fade to Black: The Negro in American Film, 1900–1942*. New York: Oxford University Press.

Dyer, Richard. 1997. *White*. New York: Routledge.

Erigha, Maryann. 2016. "Do African Americans Direct Science Fiction or Blockbuster Franchise Movies? Race, Genre, and Contemporary Hollywood." *Journal of Black Studies* 47(6):550–69.

Galuppo, Mia. 2017. "3 Female Screenwriters on Crashing the Blockbuster Boys Club: 'I Want to See a Female Darth Vader'": *The Hollywood Reporter*. Retrieved December, 2017 (www.hollywoodreporter.com/news/3-female-screenwriters-crashing-blockbuster-boys-club-i-want-see-a-female-darth-vader-1063482).

Hickey, Walt, Ella Koeze, Rachael Dottle and Gus Wezerek. 2017. "We Pitted 50 Movies against 12 New Ways of Measuring Hollywood's Gender Imbalance": *FiveThirtyEight.com*. Retrieved December, 2017 (https://projects.fivethirtyeight.com/next-bechdel/).

Johnson, Jennifer A. 2011. "Mapping the Feminist Political Economy of the Online Commercial Pornography Industry: A Network Approach." *International Journal of Media & Cultural Politics* 7(2):189–208.

King, Neal. 2010. "Old Cops: Occupational Aging in a Film Genre." Pp. 57–81 in *Staging Age: The Performance of Age in Theatre, Dance, and Film*, edited by V. B. Lipscomb and L. Marshall. New York: Palgrave Macmillan.

Kokas, Aynne. 2017. *Hollywood Made in China*. Berkeley: University of California Press.

Lindsey, Shelley Stamp. 1996. "Is Any Girl Safe? Female Spectators at the White Slave Films." *Screen* 37(1):1–15.

Lopez, Qiuana and Mary Bucholtz. 2017. "How My Hair Look?." *Journal of Language and Sexuality* 6(1):1–29.

Manatu, Norma. 2003. *African American Women and Sexuality in the Cinema*. Jefferson, NC: McFarland.

Mulvey, Laura. 1975. "Visual Pleasure and Narrative Cinema." *Screen* 16(3):6–18.

Negra, Diane. 2001. *Off-White Hollywood: American Culture and Ethnic Female Stardom*. Abingdon, UK: Routledge.

Peterson, Susan Rae. 1977. "Coercion and Rape: The State as a Male Protection Racket." Pp. 360–71 in *Feminism and Philosophy*, edited by M. Vetterling-Braggin, F. Elliston and J. English. Savege, MD: Rowman & Littlefield.

Phillips, Kendall R. 1998. "Unmasking Buffalo Bill: Interpretive Controversy and the Silence of the Lambs." *Rhetoric Society Quarterly* 28(3):33–47.

Russo, Vito. 1987. *The Celluloid Closet: Homosexuality in the Movies*. New York: Harper Collins.

Sandler, Kevin S. 2007. *The Naked Truth: Why Hollywood Doesn't Make X-Rated Movies*. New Brunswick, NJ: Rutgers University Press.

Saraiya, Sonia. 2016. "Jill Soloway on 'Transparent' Season 3, Future of Feminism and Confronting Privilege": *Variety*. Retrieved August, 2017 (http://variety.com/2016/tv/news/transparent-season-3-jill-soloway-female-gaze-feminist-theory-transgender-intersectionality-1201867529/).

Simon, David. 2008. "The Escalating Breakdown of Urban Society across the Us": *The Guardian*. Retrieved August, 2017 (www.theguardian.com/media/2008/sep/06/wire).

Smith, Stacy L., Marc Choueiti and Katherine Pieper. 2017. "Inequality in 900 Popular Films": University of Southern California: Media Diversity & Social Change Initiative. Retrieved August, 2017 (https://annenberg.usc.edu/sites/default/files/MDSCI_Race_Ethnicity_in_500_Popular_Films.pdf).

Springer, Kimberly. 2007. "Divas, Evil Black Bitches, and Bitter Black Women: African-American Women in Postfeminist and Post-Civil Rights Popular Culture." Pp. 249–76 in *Interrogating Postfeminism: Gender and the Politics of Popular Culture*, edited by Y. Tasker and D. Negra. Durham, NC: Duke University Press.

Stabile, Carol A. 2009. ""Sweetheart, This Ain't Gender Studies": Sexism and Superheroes." *Communication and Critical/Cultural Studies* 6(1):86–92.

Stokes, Melvyn. 2007. *D.W. Griffith's* The Birth of a Nation: *A History of the Most Controversial Motion Picture of All Time*. Oxford: Oxford University Press.

Tillet, Salamishah. 2018. "'Black Panther' Brings Hope, Hype and Pride": *The New York Times*. Retrieved February, 2018 (www.nytimes.com/2018/02/09/movies/black-panther-african-american-fans.html).

Whitney, E. Oliver. 2017. "Why Hollywood Needs Trans Actors: An Open Letter": *ScreenCrushNews*. Retrieved August, 2017 (http://screencrush.com/trans-actors-our-hollywood-video-glaad/).

Williams, Linda. 1989. *Hard Core: Power, Pleasure, and the "Frenzy of the Visible."* Berkeley: University of California Press.

Wood, Amy Louise. 2011. *Lynching and Spectacle: Witnessing Racial Violence in America, 1890–1940*. Berkeley: University of North Carolina Press.

Yuen, Nancy Wang. 2017. *Reel Inequality: Hollywood Actors and Racism*. Rutgers University Press.

5

DEBATES OVER
DEMEANING DEPICTIONS

Fears of Harm

Ill effects of entertainment have worried publics since the rise of media: early newspapers, novels, and libraries made such tales available to working-class children, prompting fears of waves of crime (Starker 1989). The rise of the Hollywood feature film a century ago raised new dread with its moving, often racist tales of young white women subject to raping and pimping by men. Crusades against gangster movies, and pornography per se, ensued over the course of the century, voicing fears of degradation and of violent crimes as well. More recently, marginal groups of consumers have complained of exclusion from the ranks of actors who play heroes and figures of respect, demeaned by menial roles and barred from stardom in the video age.

Producers of infamous video sometimes rise to defend their work, as at least harmless if not as morally sound. Some even apologize. In this chapter, we survey such ripostes, to show how central control of production shaped debates over the misogyny, racism, and trans- and homophobia described in previous chapters. We also show how gender and race on screen have changed with the decentralizing shift in video marketing. As patrons and fans connect online, they have changed the way producers cast and market their stories.

In 1915, however, the Supreme Court of the U.S. ruled that its film industry was mere commerce in arts and entertainment, not a political actor whose speech deserved defense (Jowett 1989). A period of regulation and censorship began in earnest, and studios had to fight distribute provocative films widely enough to profit. They built a marketing strategy with two prongs, each designed to ingratiate them to the lobbyists most likely to call for censorship. On one side, filmmakers pushed ideals of high art and free speech, claiming that movies incited reflection, not disorder, and traded in art and history rather than vice and crime (Grieveson 1997; Staiger 1990). They argued that they could illustrate the very claims that crusaders made, depicting as evil the harms that crusaders sought to stop, thus providing exposés rather than fanning the flames of crime. On the other side, Hollywood marketers staved off censorship by adopting a production code that forbade any hint of whatever spectacles the crusaders feared most: interracial sexuality or homosexuality on screen (the ban of which drove more casting of white actors in black and yellow face), and even nonsexual nudity and spouses in bed (Bernstein 1999).

This two-sided approach lasted in the U.S. until the changes of the late 1960s, when black power, second-wave feminist, and gay rights movements arose to celebrate the very freedoms that conservative crusaders had sought to repress. Since then, aspiring censors have posed less of a threat, and images of bloodshed, racial rebellion, and sexual deviance have enjoyed more freedom. Pornography exploded as an independent industry, and violence is now a staple of video conflict. We saw the consequences for images on screen in the previous chapter, and here focus on the controversies that such new stories and images breed.

Science of the effects of such media on impressionable viewers expanded as broadcast television spread through wealthy nations, right alongside the racial and sexual freedoms that conservatives opposed. Antiviolence crusaders feared the upshots for post-WWII baby boomers who watched battles every day: shootouts in westerns and cop shows, looney violence in cartoons. And while lab experiments using concentrated doses of violent footage revealed short-term excitement that would quickly fade, any hikes in rates of real-world crimes that stem from viewing have yet to appear (Savage 2008). The spread of violence on television and video games, and of pornography on the internet, paced large drops in crime, suggesting that ill effects of fiction on screen may be small. Because violence is largely situational, resulting from interactions between people off screen in real life (Collins 2008), and because most video consumption requires sitting and staring at screens rather than rising to combat, crusaders against video violence may have exaggerated their claims of its harm.

We see the opposite in research on group pride, where instead of overstating the effects of video viewing, studies may understate them instead. Survey measures of the effect of television-watching on feelings toward viewers' own racial groups (Tukachinsky, Mastro, and Yarchi 2015, 2017) yield modest but statistically significant correlations. Bursts of shared pride are probably as *situational* as violence tends to be, arising during rituals focused on symbols of our groups, the very situation of movie-going. For instance, in a viral video spread through Twitter in December of 2017, a black movie-goer shared such a moment (Colston 2017). His cell phone captures a small crowd of patrons in a cinema lobby as they look with obvious glee upon a one-sheet poster for 2018's *Black Panther*. "This is what white people get to feel like ALL THE TIME?!!!!", one says, of the joint embrace of the collage of strong, proud, black superheroes before them on the wall. A century of pushing black performers to the side increased the frequency of such rituals for whites, making them rare for blacks in cinemas. A cell phone recorded what surveys rarely can, the immediate effect of movie-going on the feelings of a group.

We mean not to dismiss well-crafted surveys of longer-term effects, as those done by Tukachinskey et al., but rather to note that lab experiments and nation-wide polling are more effective at simplifying social life and easing the collection of data than at capturing the situational nature of violence and solidarity. Crimes result from assemblies of victims, perpetrators, means, and absences of restraint, situational elements often missing from moments of movie watching and internet surfing. Shared emotions, by contrast, come from rituals. In situational terms, then, we expect movie-going and television-watching to foster little violence, but as rituals they produce plenty of common mood. Social research done far from those situations may have exaggerated video effects on crime and underplayed those on group pride and shame.

Whatever the evidence, many onlookers have worried that new depictions of gender and sex could lead to both degradation and crime. Early in the second wave of the feminist movement, for instance, small groups of activists, who fought to end violence against women, gathered to protest U.S. releases of such movies as *Snuff* (1976) and *I Spit on Your Grave* (1978). Both movies focused on real-world violations of white women and were marketed as exploitation rather than as crusader exposés (Brottman 1997; Clover 1992). Those mid-1970s protests targeted only small-scale, independent distributors, creating no problems for major studios, whose central control over the industry went unchallenged.

Over the next several years, feminist legal activists Dworkin (1981) and MacKinnon (1993) argued that heterosexual pornography, with its focus on white women subject to sexual penetration by all manner of men and other objects, was better understood as action than as speech, as degradation and violation of women than as protected expression. They held that recruiting women who find the sex distasteful, posing them in tableaux that embarrass, penetrating them in ways that can hurt, literally stigmatizing them with the bodily fluids of men, and subjecting them to violence beyond that, both enact those humiliations during photography and encourage imitative assaults on others by men who consume the porn. They urged that such video be stricken from the realm of protected speech and condemned as both record of and incitement to trafficking and crime. They were influential enough to have inspired a local ordinance against porn in the early 1980s (Alilunas 2016:178–80).

Representing the free-speech side of feminism, Judith Butler countered that, unlike the burning of a cross outside a black family's home, fictional depiction of sex cannot count as incitement to crime, because it does not distinguish any criminal or victim and never specifies any response (1997:56–7, 65–9). Patrons of porn respond in ways diverse enough to prevent states from treating it as criminal solicitation. Others point out that many women in sex work are content as professionals and bear respect as workers rather than presumption that they are victims of trafficking or complicit in crime (Bernstein 2012; Griffith, Mitchell, Hart, Adams, and Gu 2013). Still others argue that diverse pornographies serve as vital culture for sexual minorities and that regulations of them have censored liberatory speech and amounted to persecution (Rubin 1984:270–3).

As feminists debated, a larger panic over horror marketed to kids led to lawsuits over such films as *Natural Born Killers* (1994), with its scenes of the sexual predation on white women. A crusade against misogyny toward black women in hip-hop music and its accompanying videos even erupted in the U.S., focused as it was on rap's celebration of defiance and crime among black men (Miller-Youngv2007). By this time, an evangelical Christian movement took advantage of the growing internet to establish public faces of watchdog groups, linked to rightist politicians that sought the voter support that those churches could generate. Their crusader websites rated films in terms of offensive content and often threatened to lobby their politicians in favor of tighter regulation (King 2011:50–7). Those protests against video and hip-hop were large enough, involving politicians as well as organized pressure groups, to threaten to unravel Hollywood public relations and bring censorship back.

Central control over all forms of distribution and marketing had helped major studios weather storms over the racial, sexual victimization of women for a century. Their production codes and family-oriented rating systems constrained the violence and nudity that might draw censorship (Prince 2003; Sandler 2007); and their ownership of mass-media outlets allowed them to ignore other complaints, or at least reply to them in a few press interviews but otherwise bar them from marketing. For instance, filmmakers can include both the electronic press kits made to impress professional critics, and their narration of movies on running commentaries, on the home-video discs that became popular in the 1980s and 90s (Brookey and Westerfelhaus 2002).[1] In those realms, they need not rehearse any damaging controversy, and can entertain only those accusations that amuse them or at least allow them to tout their art. Neither the rise of television, the growth of cable outlets, nor the birth of home video loosened the central control that allowed filmmakers to pick and choose the accusations to which they replied.

However, as we showed in Chapter 3, social-media platforms afford long-ignored groups of consumers, such as queer, transgender, and/or nonwhite people, ways to air their views to larger groups. They can denounce films that studios wish to sell to them in ever more public ways. As the first medium both to reach a wide audience and to escape central control of corporations, peer-to-peer channels on the internet and through cell phone networks have raised hopes for greater inclusion of consumers' voices, forcing major studios to reply and even sometimes to apologize for ill effects on group pride. In her review of potentials for change in race and gender representation, Maryann Erigha (2015) notes that

> As more people drift to the Internet and alternate models of distribution for media content, Hollywood decision-makers might be compelled to incorporate a more diverse group of cultural creators in order to maintain dominance in the face of greater competition for audience attention.
>
> (88)

We illustrate these patterns in conflict over gender, sexuality, race, and other inequalities on screen by reviewing a few cases of defenses against charges of sexism and gratuitous violence that date mainly from the end of the last century. We then turn to more recent scandals over casting decisions, which have drawn fewer defenses and more open apologies and promises to change. Though the effects of these apologies on trends in hiring have yet to appear, the discourse itself has certainly changed.

Spinning Misogyny

Hollywood developed the feature film as a medium of entertainment around the specter of white women in sexual peril (in the "white slavery" movies of a century ago), and has more recently incorporated images of black women as well. Many have worried about how viewers might respond to such stories. When crusaders object to the inflammatory content exploited for entertainment, filmmakers sometimes entertain the accusations.

Celebrity responses assume certain patterns and forms, ranging from denunciations of those who accuse them to outright apologies (Benoit 1995, 1997). We next summarize the three main forms of voluntary filmmaker defense made popular over the course of the twentieth century, before turning to the changes that the television industry and internet appear to have wrought as filmmakers find themselves dragged into controversies that they cannot as easily control.

First, filmmakers accused of exploiting misogynist violence have lauded their work as art beyond the realm of ideological critique. This taps into a discourse developed a century ago during the scandalous white-slavery cycle. Says writer/director Spike Lee of a rape scene in *She's Gotta Have It* (1986), which black feminist scholar bell hooks (1996) criticized as misogynist (unless otherwise cited, we extract filmmaker defenses from their running commentaries on home-video copies of films):

> I don't think this is a feminist film. I don't think bell hooks would say it was feminist. She had an article about *She's Gotta Have It* entitled "Whose Pussy Is This?" If you have fifty women in a room,

I think that fifty women will say it's a feminist film; fifty women will say it was anti-woman. So, that's what happens with labels.

Labels, the filmmaker suggests, belong to political speech, not to art, as categories of ideology rather than personal expression. He defends his work as the creation of an artist rather than a political claim subject to fact-checking. Feminist analyses of inequality and the role of cinema in it are matters of ideology. They address people and video at the aggregate level, noting patterns across the range of product as they involve many people and movies (Haskell 1987). Indeed, we spent the previous chapter doing just that, tracking trends across decades of film and television. But filmmakers often refute such scholarly criticism as inappropriate to the individual work of video art, each with its own nuance and distinct story. Patterns in race and gender across films (upon which feminist scholarship such as our own rests) are not relevant, this argument goes. The demands of art outweigh those of factual claims and politics. In this way, Hollywood spokespeople (or, in Lee's case, an independent filmmaker hoping to secure Hollywood studio money for more high-profile films) lift their work beyond the reach of critics of the industry.

More recently, the writer of the science-fiction romance *Passengers* (2016) defended his story, in which a lonely man forces a young white woman from the life she has chosen so that he can enjoy her undivided sexual attention instead. Critics denounced the romance that develops as a Hollywood gloss on stalking, coercion, and even a kind of murder. And the writer even acknowledges "the appalling nature of our hero's actions." His defense of the romantic happy ending is

> that making a movie that leaves people room to argue about what they would have done, what they could have forgiven, what they can understand or fail to understand, I think that's great. I think that's good storytelling. . . . The movie looks, evenhandedly, at the dilemma everybody was in. I think putting good people in impossible circumstances makes for fascinating storytelling.
>
> (quoted in Lussier 2016)

From this vantage, the point of art is to consider moral questions as personal decisions (in this case, whether having trafficked a young white woman can be heroic) without taking political stances on relations between groups, to treat each character as a unique individual, unrepresentative of a larger group. The gendered politics of compulsory heterosexuality are considerations of scholars and politicians; filmmakers distance themselves from those in favor of unique works of art.

In the second form of defense, filmmakers turn around in the opposite direction and tout the *realism* of their work, which serves as exposé of the very harms against which politicians crusade. Still rebutting the 1915 Supreme Court decision, they position themselves as authors of protected political speech rather than manufacturers of products that states should govern for safety's sake. Studios learned to do this early, driven by the sheer volume of the assembly-line goods they had to sell, to differentiate their products from each other and from such consumables as, say, soap (Staiger 1990:6). This defense switches from the focus on art over politics at the heart of the first rhetoric, and embraces those politics as the noble mission served by the film. Those accused of misogyny are likely to speak in these terms when they have portrayed women as sexual victims rather than as deviants or abusers. Actress Isabella Rosselini defends the 1986 David Lynch film *Blue Velvet*, in which she plays white woman Dorothy's inability to stop a man beating and raping her.

> Sometimes they do say that David's films are misogynist. I thought of Dorothy Vallens to be opposite of misogyny. I thought it was the film that portrayed an extreme portrait of oppression of a woman. . . . All of us feel endangered because in any woman's experience there is a certain amount of abuse, whether it's light or very heavy.

More recently, defenders of routine sexual violence against white women in cable television shows resort to the same rhetoric. Says author George R.R. Martin:

> The [*Game of Thrones*] books reflect a patriarchal society based on the Middle Ages. The Middle Ages were not a time of sexual egalitarianism. . . . I wanted my books to be strongly grounded in history and to show what medieval society was like. . . . To be non-sexist, does that mean you need to portray an egalitarian society? That's not in our history. . . . Rape, unfortunately, is still a part of war today.
>
> (quoted in Hibberd 2015)

In this line of reasoning, videos that dwell on rape raise awareness of our history, and illuminate our present as well. The responsible filmmaker shows sexual aggression against women for what it is.

An actor on that show speaks of working with an organization that aides women traumatized by war (including by rape in war), and addresses fan outrage over the rape of her own character:

> I'm actually glad there was such an uproar, because there was a discussion, and that discussion is so important. We need to keep that going and keep it in the forefront of our minds and not make [the subject] such a taboo. . . . Otherwise, these women— and men—are shunned into silence. So, I think it was kind of a blessing in disguise.
>
> (quoted in Keveney 2017)

Though dispiriting to fans of strong womanhood on screen, filmmakers suggest that the use of such violence against women may lead to positive change when it drives recognition of real-world assault. Filmmakers defend their uses of rape in video entertainment by dwelling on its consequences for victims and linking that to a history worth documenting.

Where the first defense of misogyny avoids politics and lauds each work of art as unique, the second pursues the politics and declares the filmmaker to be on the right side of history, to serve an anti-rape crusade. The third rhetoric comments less on the substance than on the filmmaker's artistic intention, to shock viewers with the spectacles of such violence, and skill at realizing his intentions with his work:

> Just as there are no atheists in foxholes, there seems to be no doubt about the utility of intentionality among the producers of film. Each director wields the term with a canny sense of its potential for analysis and criticism as well as a sharply defined awareness of it limitations.
>
> (Parker and Parker 2004:20)

And though such artists might complain of unreasonable groups (especially ratings boards) misinterpreting their films in manners contrary to their intentions, they proudly take credit for how they meant to use graphic violence to shock viewers into awareness of atrocity.

For instance, *Fight Club* (1999) tells the story of a man whose attraction to a young white woman leads him both to create a fascist gang and to degrade her sexually as they date. It features several set-piece scenes of bloodshed, the most extreme of which is a vicious beating of the effeminately beautiful, young white man. The director comments that

> This is a scene that we definitely got into trouble with the censors in Britain . . . it made audiences very uncomfortable. But it's supposed to. . . . The censors came back and said, "It made us uncomfortable. We thought the fighting went on too long." And we were like, "Well, I guess we did our jobs."

In this third rhetoric, male directors assure shocked viewers of sexual violence that they intended to outrage them and used their skills to do so, and that any disgust is good for viewers.

Writer/director Paul Thomas Anderson presents his claim of mastery of his job and his viewers in the form of a cliffhanger. He tells of having screened a scene in *Boogie Nights*, in which an otherwise sympathetic male character played by Bill Macy shoots his cheating wife and her illicit lover to death, and then shoots himself as well.

Anderson recounts that he at first feared losing control of the film's audience to mass misogyny as they celebrated the killing of the adulterous woman:

> this crowd of college kids cheers when he gets the gun. Now, I sank in my seat, you know? . . . And then he shoots them, and [the viewers] cheer, even louder, and I sank even further in my seat and I thought, "Well, I have fucked up, big-time. I have ruined this. How did this happen? And how do I- and- and- I can't possibly fix it. This is one big, long shot." Well, then Macy walks out, and he shot himself in the face, and they shut the fuck up real quick. And they weren't laughing, and they weren't cheering, and it was dead silence. And I thought, "Good, ok. I've done my job ok. It's them that's fucked up." [laughing]

For these authors, doing the job is using their skill at shocking viewers to control the misogyny and bloodlust in which their films trade, first to stimulate feelings of aggression against women or effeminate men, and then to shut viewers up, to teach them a lesson. In the project-oriented labor market of Hollywood, filmmakers tend to laud their abilities to manipulate viewers in service of political progress. They style themselves as the artists whom you want to hire to make your next movie.

In what amounts to the '*Citizen Kane*' of such comment, writer/ director Mier Zarchi relates at length his heroism in caring for a woman whom he had found gang raped, beaten, and threatened with death in New York in the mid-1970s. He tells how driving her to the police station and then to the hospital, and defending her from unkind police led him to author the most reviled instance of the rape-revenge film cycle, 1978's *I Spit On Your Grave*. We noted small protests against this film above, which it drew from feminists with its punishing scenes of the repeated gang rape, beating, and attempted murder of the hero Jennifer, as she screams and tries in vain to flee. Left for dead but slowly recovered, Jennifer hunts the four rapists down and dispatches them in gruesome ways, smiling grimly once they're dead, as the credits roll.

Though Zarchi claims to have made this film as testament to the survival of the victim he aided, critics denounced it as exploitation and appropriation of women's accounts of rape. At the time, feminists challenged traditional notions of rape as either seduction leading to happy marriage or unhinged attack by the mentally ill. They worked to redefine rape as structural violence against women, a widespread practice that privileged men at women's expense. Zarchi regarded himself as taking women's side and lamented that the exploitation-oriented distributor had scrapped his original title, *Day of the Woman*, and sold the film on the grindhouse circuit as popcorn fare:

> In addition to giving the movie a new, sleazy title, the distributor also packaged it as an exploitation flick and consequently failed to present a true image of the tone of the picture. . . . I made this movie with the intention . . . to put you in Jennifer's place, to make you feel and experience the agony and pain that she was subjected to. Many critics . . . denounce and condemn it, 'cause it makes them sick to their stomachs. What did they expect a film about rape to be, enjoyable to watch? Maybe entertaining?

In this third form of defense of violence against women on screen, filmmakers aim to shock, to hammer their points about the murder and rape of women, to punish audiences for enjoying what they have long taken for granted. Accused of misogynist villainy, they ride the high road as skilled heroes with good intentions instead.

Each of these three rhetorics positions the filmmaker in relation to feminist or anti-violence protest: as an artist beyond its critique, in service of it with depictions of truth, or as part of protest by punishing viewers for enjoyment of vice.[2] Either way, filmmakers shrug off feminism and its concerns over gender violence as irrelevant to art, or contradict feminists by touting themselves as playing a role, raising consciousness of the abuses that women suffer in ways that others fear to do. That so many filmmakers counter feminist critics with admonishments of art, realism, and provocation suggests that they see themselves as the likely winners of such debates in the public eye. Male directors flaunt their skill at manipulating viewers, producers and actors tout the realism of depictions of misogyny, and nearly all agree that they are skilled artists or citizens whose speech ought to remain beyond the censor's control. They have been happy to defy feminists as narrow-minded prudes, as part of the promotion of their product. For decades, this defense of outrageous film dominated video marketing.

Unequal Stardom

More recently, however, objection to the racial and gendered patterns in Hollywood storytelling has gained new force. The loss of central control over mass media has made Hollywood producers more accountable than they once were to protests over their exclusion of minorities. The spread of internet fandom appears to have fostered successful complaints against the casting of young, white, heterosexual and cisgender actors in nearly all major roles.

Gendered and racial controversies over casting are matters of video **stardom**. Sociologically, star cults, or fandoms, breed excitement over the fact of shared focus and delight. Ritual fervor is contagious, leading gathered crowds to clap, cheer, smile, and scream in joy at the presence of the stars in their midst and to pay to see them on screen. Fans reach for such stars because we know that others do, and knowing this leads us to want pieces of them for ourselves: mementos, autographs, scraps of clothing, video recordings of widely treasured objects, etc. Possessing these, we savor moments of shared transcendence of mundane life (Collins 2000:30; Ferris 2007). Fandom is a group worshipping its own ability to grow excited by shared focus.

When groups exclude members from the possibility of enjoying that celebration, when they bar them from the centers of ritual focus, they deny them the solidarity and confidence that star worship can generate. They unplug those marginal groups from sources of social power, literally excluding them. Scholars call this power "vitality," the sense that one's group is doing well. Many groups largely barred from widely viewed video, or at least kept to background roles and rarely allowed to step forward as heroes or stars, may see themselves as enjoying less vitality. They often avoid video in disgust and only occasionally seek the pleasures of seeing their groups on screen (Abrams and Giles 2007).

Smith, Choueiti, and Pieper (2017:1) found all of three members of underrepresented racial or ethnic groups among Hollywood leads in 2015 and 2016. A report on women's *Star Wars* fandom notes that it takes the scraps offered by the earlier films, in which women play few and small roles, and innovates more satisfying stories:

> Women may be underrepresented in the "Star Wars" films, but the universe is so vast that female fans have been able to scrape together enough material to work with. Jessika Pava, an Asian female X-wing pilot, has just a few lines in "The Force Awakens," but on Tumblr, she has become the star of her own stories, where she strikes up a friendship with Poe and pursues a romance with Rey. It seems counterintuitive, but just a glimmer of a female figure can be quite generative for fans, who are then freed to insert their own narratives and analyses that aren't explored onscreen.
>
> (quoted in Hess 2016)

Another team of researchers (Hickey, Koeze, Dottle, and Wezerek 2017) ran movies of 2016 through a battery of tests for fairness in allocation of stardom and found, for instance, that no film both featured a Latina lead and showed that lead or other Latina character "as professional or college educated, speak[ing] in unaccented English, and . . . not sexualized." They quote a Hollywood writer on the importance of such stardom:

> I feel like we all deserve that. . . . Everybody deserves to see positive—not positive, I'm not a big fan of that word—but accurate and layered and complex images of themselves.

For this reason, voices long ignored in mass media but amplified by the internet now protest the exclusive casting that they call, respectively, **whitewashing** (the casting of white actors in roles otherwise belonging to people of color) and **pinkwashing** (the casting of straight actors as gay characters or cisgender actors as transgender characters). Other groups protest as well, such as against the casting of typically abled actors as disabled characters. Marginal groups denounce appropriations and demand time at the solitary center of group attention.

Bars keeping people of color off cinema screens were set in stone after the controversy over *The Birth of a Nation* in the 1910s. Racist depictions of violent blacks could result in costly scandal, and so many in Hollywood took this as license to avoid casting blacks in major roles at all, restricting them to background parts. After protests over racist depictions of gang members in the early 1970s' blaxploitation cycle and then the early 1990s' 'hood cycle, blacks found themselves yet again sidelined and consigned to unemployment or the low-prestige direct-to-video market (Klein 2011:184–5). Filmmakers had found early that they could sidestep potential controversy over race by rewriting pivotal roles for white actors. When they do that today, however, new protests over whitewashing can arise, and, in the internet age, filmmakers have become more inclined than before to reply.

First, some filmmakers maintain the appeal to have art removed from politics, which developed against charges of misogyny. Of the casting of a white woman in a part written as Africana in the source material, with which fans (of *Warm Bodies* 2012) were familiar, the writer defends the casting: "Personality is what matters in a character, not superficial indicators like height or hairstyle or even skin color, and the personalities of the cast all fit beautifully" (Berben 2012). The argument is **color-blind**, focused on individual personality and expression rather than on group-level inequality and ideology (Bonilla Silva 2006), excusing its maintenance of the latter by arguing that it has no bearing on art.

The producer of *Noah* (2014) offers a whites-are-the-world variation on this artistic distinction, as he mulls the likely outcome of racially inclusive casting:

> [In] a mythical story, the race of the individuals doesn't matter. They're supposed to be stand-ins for all people. Either you end up with a Bennetton ad or the crew of the Starship Enterprise. You either try to put everything in there, which just calls attention to it, or you just say, "Let's make that not a factor, because we're trying to deal with everyman."
>
> (quoted in High Calling 2014)

A similar logic appears in the most defensive account of casting a cis-gender actor as a trans character. We noted in Chapter 2 how the writer/director of the romantic comedy *Boy Meets Girl* turned to YouTube when ordinary casting agents could offer no suitable trans actor for his lead. He bucked an industry trend, toward casting cis men as trans women, when he hired a trans YouTuber instead. However, the casting of cis men as trans women was still common at that time, as with the casting of Jared Leto in *Dallas Buyers Club* (2013) and Jeffrey Tambor in *Transparent*. Increasingly, this trend has inspired protest, particularly via social media. Defenses of the practice, against such protest, include derogation of trans actors, as by Tom Hooper, director of *The Danish Girl*:

> [Cis male actor] Eddie also has this gift of emotional transparency—he takes you with him on a journey. I didn't want Lili to be othered by the movie or made to feel strange. I wanted an actor who would open up people's hearts to this character's journey and I think he has that gift.
>
> (quoted in Armitage 2015)

Echoing the color-blind logic, Hooper argues that this role is gender-blind, focused on what the individual actor can bring to it. He makes the claim to art about a character, rather than to ideological speech about a group.

One filmmaker offers a white feminist version of this, with her view that the dynamics between white people are representative of the lives of all women, even in such situations as marked by racial subordination as legal slavery. In her remake of *The Beguiled* (2017), based on a novel set during the U.S. Civil War, writer/director Coppola argues that the story is focused on "the power dynamics between men and women that are universal," and that she didn't feel that she could pay enough attention to racist slavery to do it justice, and so wrote out the novel's black women: "I didn't want to brush over such an important topic in a light way . . . because I want to be respectful to that history. . . . I feel like you can't show everyone's perspective in a story" (Bennett 2017). In her more official statement Coppola (2017) reiterated that "I felt that to treat slavery as a side-plot would be insulting."

Coppola concludes her defense of *The Beguiled* first by citing in quick succession each of the three rhetorics of art, realism, and auteurist intent, with which our analysis began: "it has been disheartening to hear my artistic choices, grounded in historical facts, being characterized as insensitive when my intention was the opposite." She then arrives at what we see as the heart of the matter, the inclusion of marginal groups in well-capitalized, broadly distributed, high-paying jobs in video industries: "I sincerely hope this discussion brings attention to the industry for the need for more films from the voices of filmmakers of color and to include more points of views and histories."

This inclusive sentiment, however much those who offer it intend to push or sacrifice for it, underlies the newer kinds of defense, to which we turn next. About half of the filmmaker replies to charges of exclusion that we found part ways with the three rhetorics of Hollywood marketing SOP reviewed above. Most of these remaining responses declaim responsibility; and a minority of them, which has grown in recent years, offer apologies and even promise not to repeat mistakes.

Several filmmakers cite demands for white stars that are out of their control, allowing them to deny responsibility for the offense by invoking the myths about the global market reviewed in Chapter 2.

As a Sony executive put it of the casting of Scarlett Johansen in *Ghost in the Shell* (2017), "we never imagined it would be a Japanese actress in the first place. . . . This [casting of a major white star] is a chance for a Japanese property to be seen around the world" (Blair 2016).

Likewise, when a disability rights organization protested the casting of a sighted man as a blind hero in 2017's *The Blind* ("We no longer find it acceptable for white actors to portray black characters. Disability as a costume needs to also become universally unacceptable."), the director responded by arguing that, "in order to greenlight an independent film, one must attract a 'name' actor for a fraction of a studio paycheck if there is to be any chance at getting the film financed" (Mailer 2017).

Also citing racial market forces beyond his control, albeit taking some of the collective blame, a white actor defends his own casting as a Semitic character in *Exodus: Gods and Kings* (2014), before returning to the note of inclusion:

> I don't think fingers should be pointed, but we should all look at ourselves and say, 'Are we supporting wonderful actors in films by north African and Middle Eastern film-makers and actors, because there are some fantastic actors out there.' . . . If people start supporting those films more and more, then financiers in the market will follow. The audience has to show financiers that they will be there, and [then] they could make a large-budget film.
>
> (quoted in Child 2014)

Such filmmakers largely cede claims to control of the production process to the (white)star-struck audiences, in a reversal of the auteurism observed previously in the defenses against charges of misogynist violence. We show in Chapter 2 that research has shown this belief about audiences to be a myth, one shown for the sham it is by the success in 2018 of the black-superhero movie *Black Panther*. Still, white producers maintained this myth for decades, using it as a screen for racist exclusion.

The final defensive response to protest from fans, one unique to casting controversies, is apology. The producers of *World Trade Center* (2006), in which the heroism of an African American soldier named Thomas is portrayed by a white actor, are reported to have "apologized to Thomas for the error, saying it was an oversight that they didn't catch until filming had already begun" (Gordon 2006).

The release of the fantasy epic *Gods of Egypt*, starring a white cast, likewise featured apologies from producers and the film's director:

> We recognize that it is our responsibility to help ensure that casting decisions reflect the diversity and culture of the time periods portrayed. In this instance we failed to live up to our own standards of sensitivity and diversity, for which we sincerely apologize. Lionsgate is deeply committed to making films that reflect the diversity of our audiences. We have, can and will continue to do better.
>
> (Stone 2015)

This new tendency extends to other groups as well, such as LGBTQ people long excluded and maligned in cinema. Recent years have seen not only greater inclusion of queer characters, but overt celebration of this by producers anxious to take credit for the progress and align with a consumer group. Some of this shift owes to increased participation in production of groups long excluded, as we saw in previous chapters.

For instance, the long-term Hollywood practice of killing off gay characters (see Vito Russo's "Necrology" at the end of *The Celluloid Closet*, 1987) has recently become a point of widespread rebuke, in an internet and billboard campaign against the tendency to "bury your gays." Same-sex union shortly precedes death by stray bullet for a queer character in a winter 2016 episode of the popular television series *The 100* (2014–). In a relatively early example of this pattern on television, *Buffy the Vampire Slayer* (1997–2003) had killed off a member of a long-term and recently-reunited lesbian couple, also by stray bullet, in 2002. At that time, enduring lesbian relationships were rare on television, though just as subject to flying pieces of lead; the series' creator Joss Whedon was given much credit for the pioneering work with starring characters. The scripted murder shocked and disappointed fans but led to neither mass protest nor any apology from Whedon.[3]

By 2016, fans demanded more, at least a comparable proportion of happy endings and star-making time on screen, rather than random violence to queer couples and returns to the margins. Under weeks of pressure from the fast-growing internet campaign, the writer of *The 100* offered his apology for killing the show's lesbian. His statement first gives voice to the liberal/individualist artistic distinction from which color-blind racism and other forms of discrimination emerge:

> It doesn't matter what color you are, what gender identity you are, or whether you're gay, bi or straight. The things that divide us as global citizens today don't matter in this show. And that's the beauty of science-fiction. We can make a point without preaching. We can say that race, sexuality, gender and disability should not divide us. We can elevate our thinking and take you on a helluva ride at the same time.
>
> (Rothenberg 2016)

By way of apology, the writer then notes that such principled liberal blindness does marginal groups no good:

> But I've been powerfully reminded that the audience takes that ride in the real world—where LGBTQ teens face repeated discrimination, often suffer from depression and commit suicide at a rate far higher than their straight peers. Where people still face discrimination because of the color of their skin. Where, in too many places, women are not given the same opportunities as men, especially LGBTQ women who face even tougher odds.

As fans grow more militant in demanding to see members of their groups among the stars, so do some actors. Two Asian-American players quit the television series *Hawaii Five-0* to make a point about the pay differences between them and their white counterparts (Koblin 2017). Likewise, trans women among actors have denounced the casting of cisgender men. Online protests followed the announcement that cismale actor Matt Bomer would play the role of a trans woman in *Anything* (2017). Many took to Twitter, to express not only their disappointment in the casting, but also fear of its likely outcomes. As transgender writer, actress, and producer Jen Richards tweeted, "When @MattBomer plays a trans sex worker, he is telling the world that underneath it all, trans women like me are still really just men" and "Dear @MarkRuffalo & @MattBomer: if you release this movie, it will directly lead to violence against already at risk trans women," implying as it does that trans women are really men in drag, a perception associated with often lethal violence against trans women. Following the writers of *The 100*, a producer took the apologetic (though not uncritical) route, offering in successive tweets:

> To the Trans community. I hear you. It's wrenching to you see you in this pain. I am glad we are having this conversation. It's time.
>
> The movie is already shot and Matt poured his heart and soul into this part. Please have a little compassion. We are all learning.
>
> (quoted in McNary 2016)

The process of reclaiming such roles for trans women may have reached its climax with the departure of cis male star Jeffrey Tambor from the title role in the feminist and trans-friendly television series *Transparent*, over accusations that he had sexually harassed trans women on the production of that show. As star, Tambor had collected two Emmy awards for his acting, and acknowledged the

privilege that he and his larger group enjoyed in his second accep-
tance speech in 2016:

> Please give transgender talent a chance. Give them auditions.
> Give them their story. Do that. And also, one more thing, I would
> not be unhappy were I the last cisgender male playing a female
> transgender on television. We have work to do.

Allegations that Tambor had succumbed to the Hollywood tempta-
tions to use his stardom to subordinate others arose with the late 2017
wave of accusations of sex harassment, and led to his removal from the
show. As of early 2018, the largely trans crew of this series works to
reclaim the show and carry on. As a trans writer on the staff put it in
her Instagram post, "we cannot let trans content be taken down by a
single cis man" (ourladyj 2017).

Use of social media by both fans and producers of video has spread
and seems to have altered official replies to complaints of exclusion,
from the silence or defiance that such concerns drew in the days of
greater central control, to more recent excuses that the most privileged producers do not control their own work, and even to apologies
today. Though we lack data to test the theory, it remains possible, and
probably much on the minds of filmmakers, that public acknowledge-
ment of "whitewashing" may have lowered profits for such films as *The
Great Wall* (2016, featuring Matt Damon in ancient China) and *Ghost
in the Shell*, based on the famous manga. In 2017, a white male actor
cast in an Asian role (in a remake of *Hellboy*) announced that he was
quitting that project, distancing himself from whitewashing at the
expense of a valuable job and at the risk of alienating any producers
who may value loyalty to the industry over principles of racial justice
(Sun 2017). As consumers become better organized and attentive to
online critiques of video, even the most centrally controlled producers
and actors who work for them must increasingly take note.

Such apologies were unforthcoming during the days of central control over marketing, the classical and early-blockbuster eras

documented by Russo's necrology of the queer characters buried in so many Hollywood films. Only with recent developments have producers of video found themselves accountable to groups long ignored by the star-making machinery of feature films and television series. We have mentioned two of those in this book: the rise of internet campaigns, staged by activists in public, with the wide reach and permanence that many internet sites offer; and the influx of marginal groups to television production as it expanded in the streaming-service era.

As we saw in the previous chapters, variations on the racial and gendered plotting of early Hollywood cinema transcend mere white/male fantasy and appropriation when long-excluded groups take control of production. Employment patterns matter to the look of gender on video. Likewise, to benefit from an employment-based economy, people must either be paid living wages or depend upon those who are. Professional actors need work, such that exclusion from the ranks of paid actors, never mind stars, is a matter of inequality. As trans actor Richards (2016) put it, "[Having cis men play trans women] denies actual trans women opportunities, jobs, resources, which hurts entire community." Raising wages, expanding opportunities, and reducing inequities will take collective struggle, aided by the social media that allow marginal groups both to publicize video of their own and to demand changes in the corporate product that can lift them to the heights of stardom.

We next look at the pressure that fans organized through the internet, as well as conventions, bring to bear on producers of a cult television show, to complete our picture of the increasing mixture of production and consumption in gendered video.

Notes

1   Brookey and Westerfelhaus examine an amusing commentary by prominent director David Fincher (*Se7en*, *Gone Girl*), in which he resists the widespread audience sense that the two male heroes of *Fight Club* form a homoerotic couple, "Ozzie and Harriet" as the protagonist calls them. Hollywood filmmakers have tried to shape public perception of their movies, to avoid stigmatizing controversies that might limit the size of their fandoms.

2   Not all accused of exploiting gender violence follow these three rhetorical paths. Some bear blame for causing particular filmgoers to do particular, widely publicized crimes; then they respond not with defenses of their work but with outright denials instead. For example, feminist director Mary Harron gave pre-release statements that the infamous source novel for her movie *American Psycho* had not inspired the misogynist violence of a Canadian serial rapist and killer of women (2000, p. 2.13). Filmmakers rarely respond to such charges in their promotional materials. Neither the immolations of U.S. citizens that followed similar scenes in *Fuzz* (1972) and *Money Train* (1995), the gang rapes of women by men reported after the release of *A Clockwork Orange* in England during the early 1970s, nor the American spree shootings that accompanied *Natural Born Killers* in the mid-1990s entered Hollywood's promotional discourse. Perhaps on the advice of counsel, filmmakers rarely seek marketing buzz in these scandals.

3   Whedon reportedly offered as defense that he focused his writing on male violence and dominance and didn't anticipate the demoralizing effect of Tara's murder on her queer fans (Matthewman 2003).

References

Abrams, Jessica R. and Howard Giles. 2007. "Ethnic Identity Gratifications Selection and Avoidance by African Americans: A Group Vitality and Social Identity Gratifications Perspective." *Media Psychology* 9(1):115–34.

Alilunas, Peter. 2016. *Smutty Little Movies: The Creation and Regulation of Adult Video.* Berkeley: University of California Press.

Armitage, Hugh. 2015. "Tom Hooper Confronts Danish Girl Casting Controversy": *digitalspy.com.* Retrieved August, 2017 (www.digitalspy.com/movies/news/a775929/tom-hooper-confronts-the-danish-girl-casting-controversy/).

Bennett, Alanna. 2017. "Sofia Coppola Says "the Beguiled" Is About the Gender Dynamics of the Confederacy, Not the Racial Ones": *BuzzFeed.com.* Retrieved July 20, 2017 (www.buzzfeed.com/alannabennett/sofia-coppola-beguiled-power-dynamics).

Benoit, William L. 1995. *Accounts, Excuses, and Apologies: A Theory of Image Restoration Strategies.* Albany, NY: State University of New York Press.

Benoit, William, L. 1997. "Hugh Grant's Image Restoration Discourse: An Actor Apologizes." *Communication Quarterly* 45(3):251–67.

Berben, Vanessa. 2012. "Isaac Marion's Warm Bodies Will Change How You See Zombies Forever." *Huffington Post.com.* Retrieved 2017 (www.huffingtonpost.com/vanessa-becknell/isaac-marions-warm-bodies_b_1424478.html).

Bernstein, Elizabeth. 2012. "Carceral Politics as Gender Justice? The 'Traffic in Women' and Neoliberal Circuits of Crime, Sex, and Rights." *Theory and Society* 41(3):233–59.

Bernstein, Matthew. 1999. "A Tale of Three Cities: The Banning of Scarlet Street." Pp. 157–85 in *Controlling Hollywood: Censorship and Regulation in the Studio Era*, edited by M. Bernstein. New Brunswick, NJ: Rutgers University Press.

Blair, Gavin J. 2016. "Scarlett Johansson in 'Ghost in the Shell': Japanese Industry, Fans Surprised by 'Whitewashing' Outrage": *The Hollywood Reporter*. Retrieved July 20, 2017 (www.hollywoodreporter.com/news/scarlett-johansson-ghost-shell-japanese-885462).

Bonilla-Silva, Eduardo. 2006. *Racism without Racists: Color-Blind Racism and the Persistence of Racial Inequality in the United States*. Lanham, MD: Rowman & Littlefield Publishers.

Brookey, Robert Alan and Robert Westerfelhaus. 2002. "Hiding Homoeroticism in Plain View: The *Fight Club* DVD as Digital Closet." *Critical Studies in Media Communication* 19(1):21–43.

Brottman, Mikita. 1997. "'Where Life Is Cheap"—Snuff in South America, Slaughter on Cielo Drive." Pp. 89–105 in *Offensive Films: Toward and Anthropology of Cinema Vomitif*. Westport, CT: Greenwood Press.

Butler, Judith P. 1997. *Excitable Speech: A Politics of the Performative*. New York; London: Routledge.

Child, Ben. 2014. "Christian Bale Defends Ridley Scott over Exodus 'Whitewashing'": *The Guardian*. Retrieved January 10, 2017 (www.theguardian.com/film/2014/dec/09/christian-bale-defends-ridley-scott-exodus-whitewashing).

Clover, Carol J. 1992. *Men, Women, and Chain Saws: Gender in the Modern Horror Film*. Princeton, NJ: Princeton University Press.

Collins, Randall. 2000. "Situational Stratification: A Micro-Macro Theory of Inequality." *Sociological Theory* 18(1):17–43.

Collins, Randall. 2008. *Violence: A Micro-Sociological Theory*. Princeton, NJ: Princeton University Press.

Colston, Lee Edward. 2017. "This Is What White People Get to Feel Like All the Time?!!!!": *Twitter*. Retrieved January, 2018 (https://twitter.com/LeeColston2/status/942986177191317505).

Coppola, Sofia. 2017. "Sofia Coppola Responds to 'the Beguiled' Backlash—Exclusive": *IndieWire.com*. Retrieved July 20, 2017 (www.indiewire.com/2017/07/sofia-coppola-the-beguiled-backlash-response-1201855684/).

Dworkin, Andrea. 1981. *Pornography: Men Possessing Women*. New York: Perigee Books.

Erigha, Maryann. 2015. "Race, Gender, Hollywood: Representation in Cultural Production and Digital Media's Potential for Change." *Sociology Compass* 9(1):78–89.

Ferris, Kerry O. 2007. "The Sociology of Celebrity." *Sociology Compass* 1(1):371–84.

Gordon, Ed. 2006. "Oliver Stone's 'Trade Center' Casting Recall": *National Public Radio*. Retrieved January 10, 2017 (www.npr.org/templates/story/story.php?storyId=5689104).

Grieveson, Lee. 1997. "Policing the Cinema: Traffic in Souls at Ellis Island, 1913." *Screen* 38(2):149–71.

Griffith, James D., Sharon Mitchell, Christian L. Hart, Lea T. Adams and Lucy L. Gu. 2013. "Pornography Actresses: An Assessment of the Damaged Goods Hypothesis." *The Journal of Sex Research* 50(7):621–32.

Harron, Mary. 2000. "The Risky Territory of American Psycho." *New York Times* Pp. 13.

Haskell, Molly. 1987. *From Reverence to Rape: The Treatment of Women in the Movies*. Chicago: University of Chicago Press.

Hess, Amanda. 2016. "How Female Fans Made 'Star Wars' Their Own": *The New York Times*. Retrieved August, 2017 (www.nytimes.com/2016/11/06/movies/how-female-fans-made-star-wars-their-own.html).

Hibberd, James. 2015. "George R.R. Martin Explains Why There's Violence against Women on 'Game of Thrones'": *Entertainment Weekly*. Retrieved July 20, 2017 (http://ew.com/article/2015/06/03/george-rr-martin-thrones-violence-women/).

Hickey, Walt, Ella Koeze, Rachael Dottle and Gus Wezerek. 2017. "We Pitted 50 Movies against 12 New Ways of Measuring Hollywood's Gender Imbalance": *FiveThirtyEight.com*. Retrieved December, 2017 (https://projects.fivethirtyeight.com/next-bechdel/).

High Calling, The. 2014. "An Interview with 'Noah' Screenwriter, Ari Handel." *Stewardship of Creation*. Retrieved 2017 (www.theologyofwork.org/the-high-calling/blog/stewardship-creation-interview-noah-screenwriter-ari-handel).

Jowett, Garth S. 1989. "'A Capacity for Evil': The 1915 Supreme Court Mutual Decision." *Historical Journal of Film, Radio and Television* 9(1):59–78.

Keveney, Bill. 2017. "Sophie Turner Hopes 'Game of Thrones' Rape Controversy Leads to Real-World Solutions": *USA Today*. (www.usatoday.com/story/life/tv/2017/07/13/sophie-turner-takes-action-after-game-thrones-rape-controversy/472697001/).

King, Neal. 2011. *The Passion of the Christ*. New York: Palgrave Macmillan.

Klein, Amanda Ann. 2011. *American Film Cycles: Reframing Genres, Screening Social Problems, & Defining Subcultures*. Austin: University of Texas Press.

Koblin, John. 2017. "2 Asian-American Actors Leave 'Hawaii Five-0' Amid Reports of Unequal Pay": *The New York Times*. Retrieved August, 2017 (www.nytimes.com/2017/07/06/business/media/asian-american-actors-cbs-hawaii-five-0-salary-dispute.html).

Lussier, Germain. 2016. "The Writer and Director of Passengers Address the Film's Controversial Plot Point": *Gizmodo.com*. Retrieved June 15, 2017 (https://io9.gizmodo.com/the-writer-and-director-of-passengers-address-the-films-1790382739).

MacKinnon, Catharine A. 1993. *Only Words*. Cambridge, MA: Harvard University Press.

Mailer, Michael. 2017. "Blind Director Addresses Backlash over Casting Alec Baldwin and Not Disabled Actor in Lead Role": *MSN.com*. Retrieved August 5, 2017 (www.msn.com/en-us/movies/news/%E2%80%98blind%E2%80%99-director-addresses-backlash-over-casting-alec-baldwin-and-not-disabled-actor-in-lead-role/ar-BBEpBDw).

Matthewman, Scott. 2003. "Ta-Ra Tara, Hello Homophobia?": *matthewman.net*. Retrieved August, 2017 (http://matthewman.net/2003/05/08/ta-ra-tara-hello-homophobia/).

McNary, Dave. 2016. "Mark Ruffalo Responds to Matt Bomer Transgender Casting Backlash: 'I Hear You'": *Variety*. Retrieved August, 2017 (http://variety.com/2016/film/news/mark-ruffalo-matt-bomer-transgender-movie-anything-1201850624/).

Miller-Young, Mireille. 2007. "Hip-Hop Honeys and Da Hustlaz: Black Sexualities in the New Hip-Hop Pornography." *Meridians: Feminism, Race, Transnationalism* 8(1):261–92.

ourladyj. 2017. "Untitled": *Instragram*. Retrieved November, 2017 (www.instagram.com/p/BblQ4JJlrkD/?taken-at=493604).

Parker, Deborah and Mark Parker. 2004. "Directors and DVD Commentary: The Specifics of Intention." *Journal of Aesthetics and Art Criticism* 62(1):13–22.

Prince, Stephen. 2003. *Classical Film Violence: Designing and Regulating Brutality in Hollywood Cinema, 1930–1968*. New Brunswick, NJ: Rutgers University Press.

Richards, Jen. 2016. "I Auditioned for This. I Told Them They Shouldn't Have a Cis Man Play a Trans Woman: They Didn't Care": *Twitter.com*. Retrieved June 22, 2017 (https://twitter.com/SmartAssJen/status/769927554778095618).

Rothenberg, Jason. 2016. "The Life and Death of Lexa": *Medium.com*. Retrieved August, 2017 (https://medium.com/@jrothenberg/the-life-and-death-of-lexa-e461224be1db).

Rubin, Gayle. 1984. "Thinking Sex: Notes for a Radical Theory of the Politics of Sexuality." Pp. 267–319 in *Pleasure and Danger: Exploring Female Sexuality*, edited by C. S. Vance. Boston: Routledge & Kegan Paul.

Russo, Vito. 1987. *The Celluloid Closet: Homosexuality in the Movies*. New York: Harper Collins.

Sandler, Kevin S. 2007. *The Naked Truth: Why Hollywood Doesn't Make X-Rated Movies*. New Brunswick, NJ: Rutgers University Press.

Savage, Joanne. 2008. "The Role of Exposure to Media Violence in the Etiology of Violent Behavior: A Criminologist Weighs In." *American Behavioral Scientist* 51(8):1123–36.

Smith, Stacy L., Marc Choueiti and Katherine Pieper. 2017. "Inequality in 900 Popular Films": University of Southern California: Media Diversity & Social Change Initiative. Retrieved August, 2017 (https://annenberg.usc.edu/sites/default/files/MDSCI_Race_Ethnicity_in_500_Popular_Films.pdf).

Staiger, Janet. 1990. "Announcing Wares, Winning Patrons, Voicing Ideals: Thinking About the History and Theory of Film Advertising." *Cinema Journal* 29(3):3–31.

Starker, Steven. 1989. *Evil Influences: Crusades against the Mass Media*. New Brunswick: Transaction Publishers.

Stone, Natalie. 2015. "'Gods of Egypt' Director, Studio Apologize Following Diverse Casting Controversy": *The Hollywood Reporter*. Retrieved January 10, 2017 (www.hollywoodreporter.com/news/gods-egypt-director-studio-apologize-844074).

Sun, Rebecca. 2017. "'Hellboy' Whitewashing Backlash May Signal Tipping Point for Hollywood Casting": *The Hollywood Reporter*. Retrieved September, 2017 (www.hollywoodreporter.com/heat-vision/hellboy-whitewashing-backlash-may-signal-tipping-point-hollywood-casting-1035604).

Tukachinsky, Riva, Dana Mastro and Moran Yarchi. 2015. "Documenting Portray-
als of Race/Ethnicity on Primetime Television over a 20-Year Span and Their
Association with National-Level Racial/Ethnic Attitudes." *Journal of Social
Issues* 71(1):17–38.

Tukachinsky, Riva, Dana Mastro and Moran Yarchi. 2017. "The Effect of Prime Time
Television Ethnic/Racial Stereotypes on Latino and Black Americans: A Lon-
gitudinal National Level Study." *Journal of Broadcasting & Electronic Media*
61(3):538–56.

6

FEMINIST TELEVISION AND THE POWERS OF FANDOM

On the eve of *Orphan Black*'s finale, star Tatiana Maslany told the *New York Times* that fans' "adamant vocal nature was the reason our show was anything—a success—and seen the way it was" (Koblin 2017). Over five seasons, creators and stars of this television series about cloning credited much of the success to the fans dubbed the Clone Club. That *ad hoc* community meets primarily online via such media as Twitter and Tumblr, to guess where stories will go; paint fan art and write fiction; discuss genetics, gender, and personal autonomy; and sometimes chat with producers and actors.

As we saw in the previous chapter, social networking online has given fans unprecedented ways to gain the attention of producers, to whom they make their feelings known and suggest new story-lines as well as casting. In great or small ways, fan tweets may alter television shows. Still, producers push back and defend their sense of central creative control. Early in *Orphan Black*'s run, fans began to celebrate what they saw as a feminist storyline, in which female clones defy patriarchal control of their reproductive lives; some fans demanded that showrunners follow those impulses as they wrote new scripts. This chapter explores the new forms and limits of that fan influence on studio-funded television, by focusing on pressure that feminist fans exerted over the course of the series' five seasons.

Politics aside, fans can gain producers' notice when trivia arise. During the first season of *Riverdale*, fans tweeted in jest over a character's obvious wig:

> Hopefully for season 2, #Riverdale can get a little more money in the wig budget for Clifford Blossom.

> Why does Clifford Blossom wear such an obvious wig? With his money he could afford a top of the line invisible hairpiece. #Riverdale

An executive producer later explained:

> One thing that the fans actually did affect in Season 1 was Clifford Blossom's wig. 'Cause it didn't look great. All props to our hair department, but it did not look good. . . . It was a great lesson for me cause we just leaned into it. That's where the line Hermoine says 'Clifford Blossom that wig-wearing monster' [came from]. So then we were like actually, it's more interesting if he wears a wig. It's sort of strange and Lynchian. So in that way, we definitely listened to the fans because we're fans too so we watch it in that same way.
>
> (quoted in Mason 2017)

Not only did producers write dialogue that acknowledged this fan concern, they took a step further into fan humor by giving the character a wig room.

A star of the show continues:

> With things like Twitter, we can touch base and see what they like and what they don't like. So, I think going into season 2 we really know what people are interested in. Now that we've put it out there in the world, we can expand on it and go darker and deeper.
>
> (quoted in Kinane 2017)

Twitter fans seem to have inspired *Riverdale*'s producers to make at least trivial changes to the show, humorous asides that acknowledge fan interest, along the lines of "Please Captain, not in front of the Klingons," of *Star Trek* fame. That line of dialogue appears near the end of the feature film *Star Trek V: The Final Frontier* (1989), which followed a decade of desktop-published slash fandom that depicted a romantic and sexual relationship between heroes Kirk (William Shatner) and Spock (Leonard Nimoy). Many slash fans took the obviously comic line as writer/director/star Shatner's wink at their devotional pornography.

As the final season of *Orphan Black* filmed in 2017, fans of its feminism had one last chance to air grievances in a way that could affect last-minute editing, such as lingering anger over the entry of male clones, bewilderment at the sudden disappearance of a transgender character, despair as beloved characters are shot down, and celebration of the gay life and feminism on screen. After tracking the industry forces behind the rise of feminist television, we then show how channels of fan communication have shaped both feminist reception of the show and producers' responses.

Feminist Television

Feminist storytelling on television (TV, for short) remained rare during the era of linear, ad-supported series aired by the few major networks. We reviewed in Chapter 4 the classical storyline, in which white women figure mainly as objects of male desire, protection, and possession, and as supporters of male heroes. As Lotz (2006) recounts, women have served as protagonists in small numbers of television shows since the early days of the medium, but rarely in overtly feminist stories that would challenge those classical roles. They appeared as partners of men in action dramas in the 1960s and 70s, and then alone or with other women in shows that focused on heterosexual appeal (e.g., *Charlie's Angels*, *Wonder Woman*). Evening dramas about cops and courts sometimes drew on feminist ideas about workplace harassment and sexual coercion, as in the female buddy cop series *Cagney and Lacey* (1982–88) and the legal drama *L.A. Law* (1986–94). But the telling of feminist stories remained limited by how mainstream they had to be.

Twentieth-century TV shows required audiences to watch the few available broadcasts at times set by centrally controlled networks. Fans of early seasons of *Cagney & Lacey* who hoped to catch a new broadcast had to sit in front of the television on a Monday night from 10–11 p.m. and endure regular interruptions by advertisements. They may not have been able to see the previous week's broadcast or recall events from earlier in the several-year series. Built upon the protagonist-centered storytelling of Hollywood film reviewed in Chapter 4, clear plotting required instantly recognizable characters who handled newly introduced problems with easily understood motives and gained resolution during the twenty-two or forty-four minutes of a nightly episode. This linear, mass-audience model constrained what popular video could show, narrowing it to uncontroversial stories of unchanging TV-star protagonists who address problems quickly (Lotz 2017a; Thompson 2003). Heroes faced a limited range of problems because the wide broadcasts of the few networks drew big money from advertisers who marketed to tens of millions of viewers at a time. Those in central control of marketing and distribution disliked controversies that could damage their mass-appeal brands and so restricted subversion to quick and often comical protests by otherwise contented heroes.

Consider for example an early and influential moment on a prime-time situation comedy. Aired in the fall of 1972, back when the new feminist movement struck most onlookers as either trivial or outrageous, the opening episode of the third season of *Mary Tyler Moore* staged a fight between Mary and her boss over pay. Recently promoted, Mary learns that she earns less than her male predecessor had. As an excuse, her boss notes that the man served as the family breadwinner whereas Mary lives alone. By the end of the twenty-two minute episode, Mary wins the debate over her pay by citing its sexism. The quick resolution of the matter and lack of recurrence in the five seasons that followed kept such gender disparity from becoming a theme. As actor Moore said thirty years later, of her sitcom-counterpart's status as a feminist, "She wasn't aggressive about it, but she surely was. The writers never forgot that. They had her in situations where she had to deal with it" (King 2002). The quickness with which Mary deals with it, and her ability to do so by herself, kept the show *post*-feminist.

Young fans of Mary's feminism took inspiration that shaped their own productions later, such as in Tina Fey's comically post feminist situation comedy *30 Rock* (2006–13). But the rapid disappearance of any inequality or protest against it was built into the industry at the time. Situations in which female heroes had to deal with the problems that drive feminism would arise but then resolve by the end of an episode and rarely involve any collective or time-consuming work.[1] Advertisers liked shows that featured such young career women but preferred the *post*-feminism, in which a professional like Mary feels no need to join other women in any fight against sexism. This new-woman approach to popular sitcoms and dramas increased the numbers of female protagonists decade by decade (Lotz 2006) but allowed only brief flashes of feminism.

Feminism on video requires more than a hero or two who can easily quell threats in a world that remains good in mainstream terms without undergoing any change of character. It needs a depiction of ongoing inequality, one that affects large gender groups (women, men, and those who escape or resist those categories), against which women must join to fight in longer-term struggles that change them or their world. This means social ills that buck liberal assumptions of a just world, struggles between groups larger than handfuls of heroes, and longer character arcs than strictly episodic TV could build.

The homogenizing stranglehold of major networks and their advertisers loosened with the spread of analog cable television in the 1980s and then satellite and digital cable, and digital recording devices, in the 1990s and 2000s. First, more producers targeted women's audiences. Lotz's history of U.S. production (2006) shows how female protagonists emerged first in action-adventure shows and spread into occupational dramas about cops and medical personnel over the 1980s. After Lifetime aimed its entire cable-channel roster of programs at women in 1994, a dam burst, such that the late 1990s saw a rapid growth in the number of shows centered on women, from *Buffy the Vampire Slayer* (1997–2003) to *Sex in the City* (1998–2004). The wave of women as protagonists crested at the end of the century, in a series of dramas focused on the ideal consumer whom advertisers hoped to reach: "most are white, heterosexual, single, employed in highly professionalized careers, and live in upper-middle-class, if not upper-class, worlds" (6–7).

Still, the industry shift that would allow for a critical mass of *feminist* content was a decade away. Many of these shows remained post feminist, focused more on personal loyalties between two or just a handful of women as friends. Though Lotz shows that many of the adventure series feature supernaturally gifted heroes who protect innocents from the evils of masculine foes, any sense of gender oppression tended to remain implicit or easily tossed off as humor.

The targeting of women as a diverse set of consumer audiences did not by itself lead feminism to burst onto screens. Most women are not feminist, and mass advertisement aims at the larger group. Real feminism on TV followed a second trend, the rise of creator-driven, niche-marketed shows offered by a cable channels that pursued rather than avoided political and cultural controversy. This occurred only after new technologies of distribution and recording multiplied the channels that a household could receive, from a few dozen to hundreds. They shifted business models from reliance on advertisers hoping to reach tens of millions of people to fees paid by more open-minded niche subscribers (Lotz 2017a). In this newer business model,

> The audience strategy is simply that of curating content to meet the needs of a specific audience or audience taste, especially

niches not well served by existing television. For example, Noggin provides a portal with programs for preschoolers; WWE Network features programming interesting to wrestling. . . . [S]ince the majority of portals rely on subscriber funding, the difference in revenue model requires portals to truly serve their audience niche.

(Lotz 2017b)

From Lotz's history we learn how producers can now serve niche audiences as much as mass ones, and pursue narrative innovation and diversity even to the point of the political subversion that would have kicked them off the air thirty years ago.

At the same time, proliferations of digital recording, disc rentals, and streaming channels broke the linearity of the old television model. They made it possible for viewers to gather episodes and binge-watch whole seasons in a few days or weeks and thus take in stories that involved more characters, who could change over the length of a story as they handled problems that took far longer to resolve. The arrival of streaming services through high-speed internet channels added fuel to the fires that destroyed the old linear model of television.

Only in this new era, with its new business models and machines, have expensively produced (as opposed to DIY) feminist stories reached the screen to be seen by large audiences. We show in Chapter 1 how television producers gave more high-profile coverage to women's roller derby over the middle of this decade, from streaming bouts in 2015 to live cablecasts in 2017. During the last half dozen years, producers such as Jill Soloway have likewise expanded from their relatively apolitical but pro-gay and kindly reviewed cable dramas, such as *Six Feet Under* (2001–05), to a rapidly growing set of mini-series and longer-running shows that focus on women working together under the pressure of discrimination, condescension, and even violence by men. This is a wave of feminist storytelling unprecedented in popular video: *Bomb Girls* (2012–13), *Top of the Lake* (2013–17), *Good Girls Revolt* (2015–16),

Sweet/Vicious (2016–17), *Big Little Lies* (2017–), *The Bold Type* (2017–), *GLOW* (2017–), *Godless* (2017), and *The Handmaid's Tale* (2017–). Still more series depict women's daily lives under pressure to maintain gender ideals: *United States of Tara* (2009–11), *Transparent* (2014–), *One Mississippi* (2015–17), *I Love Dick* (2016–17), and *Insecure* (2016–). This very recent but rapid expansion of feminist TV suggests that the experiments allowed by the new business model included enough successes that other producers are willing to try. Held back from screens for decades, feminist storytellers are having their day.

Orphan Black

This Canadian science fiction show arose with that young cohort of TV feminism (2013–17), focusing on a group of women who gradually assemble, change their hearts and minds, and gather strength to fight "the patriarchy." It begins when petty thief Sarah (Tatiana Maslany) stumbles onto the suicide of an identical twin she's never met. Bewildered but desperate to flee her own problems, Sarah steals the suicide's identity, only to find herself swept into a hidden struggle. She learns that her sister was not merely a twin but one of many such clones, products of a corporation run by a homicidal patriarch. For five seasons, Sarah and a growing squad of siblings recruit and support each other to battle conspiracies to breed, examine, profit from, and slaughter them.

Feminist viewers quickly cheered the show's focus on gender oppression and the fight by this rebel sorority and their crew of gay and mostly female supporters. Creators Graeme Manson and John Fawcett had not intended to include all of those politics, but were happy to follow where the casting and story took them. As Manson explains:

> We certainly didn't set out to make a feminist show. . . . The themes of the show and the embodiment of Tatiana with all these characters made the theme.
>
> (Thomas 2014)

Over the course of production, however, creators and actors began to flaunt its politics.

> Manson: [*Orphan Black*] is so thematically connected to feminist issues; who owns you, who owns your body, your biology? Who controls reproduction?
>
> (Loofbourow 2015)

> Kristian Bruun (actor): I'm really proud of the fact that it's a feminist show. It's very LGBT-positive and supportive. And I think we need to put more of those stories out there, especially right the fuck now.
>
> (Costa 2017)

By positioning several women as heroes and leaving men to fill supporting roles, *Orphan Black* portrayed women's struggles over reproductive autonomy, the policing of women's bodies, and LGBT rights. Feminism appears in video any time women or girls band in solidarity to fight gendered oppression; and, in the final season, the core group of "sestra" clones (so dubbed by a Ukrainian among them) defeat the wealthy man who exploits and threatens them. As star Maslany explains:

> [He] sort of symbolizes the head of the snake. . . . He's the top of everything and so the source of a lot of answers to the questions the clones have had for seasons, and that have put all of these people in jeopardy—and [he also] represents the patriarchal system that we're all in that seeks to control us. So that's, I guess, a theme of the season—and we've talked about that from Season 1—but we face it head-on this season.
>
> (Dershowitz 2017)

A video promoting the show's final season sounds even more like a feminist rally, as clones take turns to deliver a joint speech:

> From the very start they hunted us, controlled us, used us, betrayed us. But they could not break us, because we found each

other. We came to love each other, joined together, and vowed to protect each other. Now we fight. We decide our destinies; to control our bodies, to love whom we choose, to live our lives. Now we fight for my babies, for my sisters, for the family we've chosen, for our freedom. Together we fight with everything we've got and everything to lose. For a new future. Together we fight until the end. Together we are one.

The opposition of solidary women to oppressive manhood appears in the show's dialogue, as when the villain sneers with satisfaction over the system of lies and wealth on which he depends: "That's how the patriarchy works" (*Orphan Black*, fifth season, sixth episode).

Feminist fans posted widely of the joy of seeing their politics on screen. But they also challenged the writers over the brevity of time spent with trans, gay, and nonwhite characters, and over the introduction of male clones who competed with women for screen time. Having looked in the previous chapter at the growing power of activists to challenge Hollywood exclusion, and seeing how feminism grows with the TV industry's decentralizing shifts, we next see how much influence viewers have over feminist casting and storylines. Fans protest plotting that steals the spotlights from their most beloved female and queer stars. Did they make any difference?

The Power of Fandom

Scholarly studies of fans have focused on the ways in which marginal groups adapt mainstream fare to include or at least inspire them, for instance by "slashing" TV shows such as *Star Trek*, to make its straight or sexless male heroes into lovers (Penley 1997). Female readers of romance novels likewise take comfort in the lowbrow books, experiencing stirring feelings of being desired and loved while they toil in their unsupportive homes (Radway 2009).

Scholars of fandom call this "poaching" (Certeau 1984)—attempts by those with little mass-storytelling power to take a bit of pleasure in the pop culture than often excludes or demeans them. Poachers revise and adapt commercial images or stories to their own needs, by slashing, reediting, or otherwise turning them around.

New technologies have allowed fans to distribute their own art, with which they celebrate and alter their favorite shows, from the desktop publishing and video dubbing that empowered slash fandom, to the personal computing and internet that have allowed for explosions of the same. Scholars of fandom have tracked the emergence of these as consumer markets that producers must bear in mind and address, as we saw in the previous chapter.

However, recent studies of fans have shown how highly capitalized producers use what central control they have to keep fans out of their storytelling, shunning them to the margins of marketing instead. Indeed, as Andrejevic (2008:42) points out, poaching online as a fan of some popular video isn't "poaching" in the medieval sense at all. Peasants poached game on private lands without the lord's leave, stealing from property that he claimed, to sustain families of their own, *depriving* the legal owner rather than enriching him. Fan poachers on message boards generate marketing data for corporations and encourage each other's consumption, *enriching* owners of shows while boosting only solidarity and consumer pleasure among themselves. The financial capital goes up, not down. In economic terms, this is not poaching at all. It serves more as free labor for corporations looking to increase profits.

This raises the question of what fans can and cannot do, and how much of what they do bolsters profits of production studios instead of the hunger for respect of excluded groups. Some creators speak of shaping at least minor stories with fan feedback in mind. For example, on several occasions, I. Marlene King mentioned tweaking *Pretty Little Liars* to reward fans for their loyalty, by ensuring that their favorite couples wind up together in the series finale:

> No one ever intentionally *lurks* [a reference to reading fan posts about one's own show] for ideas. But there are times when we see a wave of interest in a certain storyline and we will give it more life, maybe, than we originally planned.
>
> (King 2014)

I do think that when you see how passionate fans get about certain things or story lines and couples, it definitely influences how
you tackle breaking the season, because you want to make sure
that fans stay happy. It probably wouldn't change the outcome
of the mystery, but it probably would change the outcome of a
couple being endgame.

(Ivie 2017)

In a rhetoric maintained across the industry, the writer distinguishes
the major plotline (outcome of the mystery in this case) from more
minor ones, such as resolutions of romances.

Likewise, Edward Burns has also been open to using Twitter as a
place for conversation with fans over his TV series:

When I was coming up with my idea for *Newlyweds* I kind of
tweeted out "What do you guys think of the idea?" And there
was an overwhelming positive response to the idea. And then, as
I started to map it out, I would just ask them questions; and they
gave me some really sort of great directions to go in.

(Renée 2013)

However, Burns speaks of constraints on fan involvement in writing,
distinguishing between fan marketing in a context of decentralized
control and niche media, and his mastery of the plot on which he rests
his reputation as an artist:

It's harder and harder for us to reach our audience . . . You need
to have a meaningful relationship with your fans, because you're
going to need them to do a lot of the marketing work that, lets
say, a studio or a record label or a book publishing company used
to do for artists in the past . . . So, I just went on Twitter. . . .
Since we finished [*Newlyweds*] we did- like- a poster contest
with them, which they really enjoyed . . . And then they came
out and not only bought the movie, but they told their friends to

buy the movie as well. So, in this age, where we have to pay for our own marketing, it's an invaluable tool.

In their intensive study of fan-producer relations over a TV show, Zubernis and Larsen (2011) explain that creator Eric Kripke had to navigate the avid fans of *Supernatural* (2005–), a community with a large presence in the online world and at conventions. Their research also suggests that producers may entertain fans and curry their favor but remain jealous of any sense of ultimate control.

Actors and showrunners of *Supernatural* voice thanks for fan support and awareness that they may shape storylines. Star Jensen Ackles has stated:

> Before all the social networking, and the tweeting and the facebook and the blogs and the posts, I'm not sure fanfavorite021 from Germany really had a voice about whether the storyline went a certain way, but it seems to me that now they do. They're getting paid attention to by the people creating the show, and that goes to the show that there's an interesting relationship forming now with the technology we have between the creators of these shows.
>
> (quoted in Zubernis and Larsen 2011:178)

Likewise, Kripke recognizes the involvement of fans in creative decisions, but only to a point. For instance, Kripke learned that a guest character, Bella, was forced onto the show by the network but collectively hated by fans. He had her written back out and chalks this decision up to "self reflection":

> We all started talking about it. I think the majority of shows have this attitude like, we know better, and we don't. We kind of examine it and see if it really works or doesn't. And with Bella, we had a hard time fitting the character into the mythology in a way that's seamless . . . every time she showed up, we had to

write up some reason, and it started to feel sort of ridiculous and artificial and inorganic to the process.

(quoted, 179)

Kripke notes fan reaction but still attributes the fate of the character to his own concerns with proper storytelling, and to his resistance to interference.

Zubernis and Larsen argue that Kripke listens with care to fans, concerned not to misunderstand complaints about misogyny and racism (180). He tells of shaping an episode in response to fan objection to casual expressions of homophobia between the straight male buddies at the center of the show. He created a brief love story involving a gay character in the spring of 2008. Nevertheless, he quickly killed that character for romantic tragedy, contributing to the "Bury Your Gays" trend reviewed in the previous chapter, which would become infamous over the subsequent years. Noting fan offense at the death of the lovestruck queer man, Kripke is defensive:

the core of the story is how love supersedes anything, and I don't get it when people say because the gay character ends up dead that it's homophobic, because the hero is a gay man, and the other character [with whom the doomed gay man is in love] is someone who comes to realize the power of love.

(quoted, 180)

Kripke listens to fans but also keeps them at some distance, arguing that fans do not want, or at least do not benefit from much control over storylines, and that any fan service winds up condemned by creators and fans alike. Though he is willing to alter a subplot to entertain his fans, the larger arc of the story remains his to shape:

As soon as you give them what they want, they're irritated that they're getting what they want, immediately after there's a burst of comments like "fans are controlling the show now." The reality of this business is this is serialized drama. I have the story I'm telling, what all the plotting and conspiracy is leading up to, and I've never deviated from that story, it's been right on since the pilot and that's what matters to me. . . . The fans don't have as much power as they think they do.

(quoted, 179–80)

Such boasting of lack of concern for fan feelings maintains both a masculine stance of lack of obligation to care—of pleasing others only when one chooses to do so—and the creative control at the heart of project-based Hollywood production. A white, male star of the show echoes that paternalism:

Padalecki: Pleasing the fans, luckily, is—I hope this doesn't sound bad, I should preface it by saying that I love my fans, but I do not care in the slightest about it. It's my job not to care. If I start trying to please the fans, then it would backfire and I'd end up not pleasing the fans.

(quoted, 184)

This pattern of inclusion in marketing but exclusion from plotting and character in mind, we can ask whether fans shape the storytelling of *Orphan Black* in ways that affect the larger exclusion of marginal groups from the stardom in which TV shows trade.

#CloneClub Controversies

Clone Club operates online as a social network, in which fans bond over their mutual love of the show. They voice devotion but sometimes dissent as well. When producers interact, fans may feel part of the creation of the show, just as industry personnel can bend those conversations to the purpose of marketing without allowing fans to alter main plots.

Orphan Black producers have often solicited Clone Club to comment on trivia rather than on storylines or representation of marginal groups as stars, hoping that members feel valued and turn their fandom to marketing, without giving them control over the storyline. For example, before the premiere of Season Four, BBC America, which airs *Orphan Black*, teamed with marketing magazine *Entertainment Weekly* to stage a contest, in which a fan's poster would become part of the marketing campaign. The winner would receive $10,000 and a private screening of the premiere (EW Staff 2016). BBC America thus made use of art that fans were already creating, at little cost to their publicity departments. The viral buzz both marketed the show and encouraged even greater loyalty among fans by making them feel part of the production, not just reception. As Barnett explained:

> We had a competition and said "we will use the fan art we select as the key art for marketing for the show." . . . We really saw it as a way to actually allow and invite the fans into the shaping of the conversation around the show.
>
> (quoted in Koblin 2017)

Of course, fans already shaped conversation around the show, which discussion was largely theirs by definition. The marketing tactic is to lend fans the impression of participating further, in production, by focusing them on marketing. Producers hope to generate more enthusiasm by doing so and use that viral spirit to boost support for the show, all without having to pay much for the labor or cede control over the stars and storylines.

In subsequent marketing stunts, producers invited fans to nominate props that might appear on the show (Figure 6.1). Such contests engage fans but remain tangential to the changes fans could potentially make to plotting and characters that shape the stardom at the center of it all.

As Barnett said, of the latter contest over props, "Fans went crazy for it and said, 'OMG, you're listening to us, we're being heard.'" Manson explained that he was okay with this type of involvement as long as BBC America and the fans "weren't putting pressure on us story-wise."

Figure 6.1 A showrunner's tweet celebrates fan input into a trivial moment of *Orphan Black*.

These things weren't affecting the direction of the show. That's another issue: When you have all that feedback, it's easy for us to see what people like and don't like. Though we're not taking direction or changing story lines necessarily, it certainly gives you a direction and it tells you what people like about characters and what they want to see from characters.

(quoted in Koblin 2017)

Fans have opined on every aspect of the show, including its nearly all-white cast. We next review three protests that have drawn repeated, highly politicized rebuke: the failure to bring transgender clone Tony back for the final season, the introduction of male clones, and the shooting of queer hero Delphine.

In a Season Two episode that aired in the summer of 2014, *Orphan Black* introduced the transgender clone Tony, to mixed reviews (Figure 6.2). Though many praised the representation in part for its rarity, some criticized it as a token and cliché. Fans mostly gave it a pass on its casting the cis female star as a trans man (a point about transphobia reviewed in Chapter 5), out of both loyalty to the star and appreciation of the show's focus on variation among the clones.

Figure 6.2 Trans male clone Tony strikes a masculine pose, barring the way of a potential lover in *Orphan Black*.

Still, many were grimly amused. As a trans* queer critic for Bitch-flicks put it, "It is, apparently, very difficult to put a good trans character in your TV show" (Thornton 2014).

Maslany acknowledged that responses varied, maintaining the general account of limits on fan influence and the artistic value of disturbing viewers:

> for as many people that are having an adverse reaction to Tony there were just as many influential people who really cared about him. I don't mean influential in any way except that he moved them in a certain way or he spoke to them because they felt represented or they felt like their friends were represented onscreen. We never set out to make a political statement or anything with Tony. It was just- we were fascinated with that exploration and expression of gender identity because our show's about identity. [Any adverse reaction from fans to a character. . .] I think that's great, we should challenge people, and there shouldn't always be

an easy response to things, or else we're not making our television show.

(quoted in Dowling 2015)

Nevertheless, creators spoke of the political weight of portraying a trans clone, in Manson's account:

> We definitely felt the responsibility of portraying this. We did a lot of work and Tatiana did a lot of work to portray this character in a way that we felt was respectful of that community but also worked within the context of our show.
>
> (quoted in Bentley 2014)

That writer also invoked the artistic distinction so popular among producers of video accused of demeaning or excluding groups:

> We looked at it as, okay, if we're going to do this, we're going to do it from exactly the right place creatively and story-telling wise and we're going to commit 100%. And as long as we move forward with our hearts in the right place, hopefully the sexual politics rise above it. That's sort of how we approached the storytelling, too. Throw the character in and treat the character exactly like you'd treat anyone else, and give them their dignity and respect.
>
> (quoted in Ross 2014)

Here, Manson sidesteps any concern about a cis woman taking the role of a trans man by asking audiences to focus on the unique story rather than any industry pattern of exclusion or cis-casting.

Dialogue in a few subsequent episodes mentioned Tony, but he remained off screen. Producers occasionally hinted at his return but never brought him back. We must speculate in what appears to be a pointed absence of producer comment; it seems likely to us that the controversies over casting cisgender actors that blew up in 2016 (see previous chapter) might have quashed any plans to bring Tony back during the final season in 2017. Moreover, the lack of producer comment strikes us as part of the larger stance of creative control that still governs public relations in video production.

In the second example of fan demand and producer response, the Season Two finale later in the summer of 2014 introduced male clones known as Castors, some of whom assault women. Writers Fawcett and Manson meant to focus on the feminist issue of men's sexual aggression:

> If you want to explore feminist themes, you have to challenge those themes. And if there's one way to highlight our feminist themes, it would be to throw a misogynist into the mix.
>
> (quoted in Goldstein 2015)

However, critics and fans alike would challenge this choice to introduce male clones to a female centric show worrying that male clones would "ruin Orphan Black" by drawing attention from the female characters (Hogan 2014; Towers and Dornbrush 2015; Tracey 2015). Fans tweeted their disappointment:

> @nongenderous: I hope all the Castor clones die in the new season of Orphan Black.
> @girlsdaylesbian: i will sacrifice my life so that no one dies in the orphan black finale tonight unless it's a castor clone

Although the creators never addressed this controversy in public, dialogue made little mention of the male clones after that third season. Later in the following season (Four), a single Castor clone appears, one said to have been raised apart from the aggressive ones and who remains servile to women rather than misogynist. In the fifth and final season, that remaining Castor dies at the hands of the woman he faithfully serves, while the four core "sestra" clones enjoy a happy ending (Figure 6.3). Again, a lack of showrunner comment leaves us to speculate why such a major plot device went missing after a wave of fan rebuke. Producers appear to learn a few lessons from fan outrage but keep silent about their decisions to alter major storylines.

Figure 6.3 Four sestras enjoy a happy ending in the conclusion of *Orphan Black*.

In the third instance of protest and reply, fans erupted over an apparent instance of the "Bury Your Gays" trope at the end of Season Three, in June of 2015. Like the creators of *The 100* a year later, *Orphan Black*'s writers and star were mindful of the long-term pattern of killing LGB characters on TV shows. The #buryyourgays twitter hashtag dates from the fall of 2013 and was well known by the time of production of Season Three in the winter of 2015. Nevertheless, showrunners featured, in that season's finale, the shooting of fan favorite Delphine. She is a scientist who has fallen in love with sestra Cosima. Fans had dubbed the queer couple Cophine. The #cophine twitter feed is full of fan art in tribute to their romance and the thrill of seeing two such women happily paired on screen.

Maslany responded defensively to fan outcry over the shooting of Delphine, by claiming the artistic distinction that we reviewed in Chapter 5:

> There's a bizarre focus on the fact that she's bisexual or a lesbian and has been killed off, and that really reduces her to one thing in representing something, as opposed to being an

individual. I find that to be a problematic complaint. She's so much more than her sexuality and to make it about, "well, we killed off a lesbian character," that's really reductive. I understand because there's such a lack of representation and 3D representation and you're protective of those characters. There's a trope too, a predictable storyline, which is that the LGBTQ characters get victimized somehow. But Delphine is only a victim because she made herself a hero. She was ultimately doing right by people.

(quoted in Anderson 2016)

Writer Manson also drew from the rhetorics reviewed in the previous chapter, invoking his status as author in control of the show's provocations, ridiculing fans for not knowing what tragedy a good story requires:

From the very beginning, we said we would constantly pull the rug out from people. If there's a backlash, we earned it. If you did everything that the fans wanted, it wouldn't be a drama anymore. There would be no mystery to it. Delphine and Cosima would just be naked in bed and that would be the show. We'd just keep cutting to them over and over and everyone would be happy, right?

(quoted in Anderson 2016)

As defensive as they were about the shooting, producers kept mum about long-term plans and eventually restored Delphine, giving the couple a happy ending in the show's conclusion.

From these three rounds of give-and-take between unhappy fans and defensive producers, we infer that the latter may try to keep fans happy to maintain support of the show, perhaps by leaving the misogynist Castors and awkward transgender clone offscreen once fan rebukes come in. They may even have given #Cophine a happier ending than they otherwise would have, though we lack evidence either way. What we do observe is that producers remain silent on or overtly disavow any changes to story arcs made to please fans. Claiming the artistic control described in Chapter 5, they reply defensively to fan complaints, even as they avoid giving further offense.

This reluctance from auteurs, to cede any control to the pull of their fans, is not new to *Orphan Black*. While fans and protestors have learned how to challenge casting exclusions, auteurs tell the difference between the main storyline and mere subplots or marketing. They appear to maintain a strong sense of ultimate control while listening to fans and involving them as marketing tools. Feminist pressure on the writers of *Orphan Black* may have killed off male clones and kept Tony off screen, but showrunners guard their senses of storytelling skill that they use to market themselves in a project-based film and television industry. Fans remain marketing tools of job-seeking artists at this point in the shift toward wider participation in popular video. Feminist pressure appears to have altered gender in video, both as showrunners find niches for their stories, and fans call producers to account for casting exclusions. Still, fan control of production appears to have reached a limit, where producers stand their ground as final arbiters of storylines.

Lastly, we note that these changes in currents never end. In early 2018, one of the most prolific producers of streaming niche television, Amazon, ordered the cancellation of two feminist shows: Diablo Cody and Tig Notaro's *One Mississippi* (2015–17) and Jill Soloway *I Love Dick* (2016–17) (Holloway 2018). Those had been developed by an executive who was later fired in the sex-harassment scandals of 2017. As one critic assessed the business strategy:

> Jeff Bezos has ordered the studio to back away from the kind of niche-y original programming they built their name on in search of broader material that performs better internationally.
>
> (Dessem 2018)

The business model that made a wave of feminist shows will give way to other models, which will continue to reshape gender on screens.

In doing so, those new models join a wave, such as the rise of national industries that can challenge the hegemony of Hollywood from such cities as Mumbai, Mexico City, Seoul, Tokyo, London, Beijing, Manila, Hong Kong, and Bangkok. As new media create new routes for money and video to follow, producers can find funding and display their wares further from the central control of Hollywood talent agencies, production firms, and major studios.

Those Hollywood worksites may as well have been engineered to maintain inequality, with their systems of informal mentoring that require members of marginal groups to hope and beg for fairness from white men who need never account for their exclusions. As Caldwell (2008:227) put it:

> The economic genius of the mentoring system is that it gives production companies great flexibilities in hiring and promotion practices. . . . Designed and justified as an enabling career process, the mentoring system also tends to exclude those who do not share the cultural identities of the company culture in question.

Decades of political protest, like the one that women began in the fall of 2017, have done little to change these systems. Their flexibility and opacity make them like rubber, able to resume their former shapes as political pressure wanes. The President of the Director's Guild assessed the reason for "the lack of women and people of color across all aspects of opportunity and employment" in 2016:

> Statements, statistics, pleas, and calls for action have done little to move the needle. It is time to be clear—structural changes

are needed. Those who control the pipeline and entryway to jobs must move beyond the "old boy" network and word-of-mouth hiring. They must commit to industry-wide efforts to find available diverse talent that is out there in abundance, or to train and create opportunities for new voices entering our industry. Rules must be implemented to open up the hiring process and rethink the idea of "approved lists."

(Barclay 2016)

In response to such inertia that year, government agency Telefilm Canada (2016) announced its intent to build "a representative and diversified feature film portfolio that better reflects Canada's population." Two months later, the agency set forth transparency policies for funding and promotion designed to take power from unaccountable managers and executives and subject them to scrutiny instead. By 2018, an internal study showed that:

The initiative already is having an effect: A 2017 Telefilm study shows a 27 percent increase in agency-backed projects directed by women since 2015. And it's not just Telefilm: The National Film Board of Canada, the Canadian Broadcasting Corp. and the Canada Media Fund also have unveiled plans to achieve gender parity by 2020.

(Vlessing 2018)

By favoring marginal groups long enough to see that members could contribute to two features, and thus claim real experience in their fields, the initiative may break longstanding barriers to hiring and promotion. If so, then it will join the series of genre booms and media inventions that have tended to open the most doors to video production. Should this occur across the world's video industries, then we might see DIY producers face less painful choices as they weigh participation in corporate broadcasting, like the skaters reviewed in Chapter 1. The women shut out of informal networking and subject to exploitation within it will find ways around the stumbling blocks that so many unaccountable white men have made of themselves. Groups long sidelined by major studios may find more work without having to incarnate white/male fantasies or appropriations. Fans tired of seeing their hero roles appropriated by dominant-group actors may find greater satisfaction, and may find showrunners and auteurs more responsive to the pressures that viewers exert. We look to such interventions to improve business as usual in the industries that produce the most star-making video.

Note

1   This storytelling form demanded speedy resolution on any shows other than daytime soap operas. Those five-day-per-week serials were infamous for spinning stories for years on end, but even so still bounced clearly distinguished characters off each other like billiard balls, each acting on distinct dispositions, the evil ones doing wrong, innocents at least trying to do right, none of them reshaped by larger forces. Lotz (2006:74) also points out that soap operas focused on contention rather than solidarity between women.

References

Anderson, Stephanie Marie. 2016. "Tatiana Maslany Responds to 'Orphan Black' Fan Backlash": *SBS TV*. Retrieved August, 2017 (www.sbs.com.au/topics/sexuality/article/2016/04/13/tatiana-maslany-responds-orphan-black-fan-backlash).

Andrejevic, Mark. 2008. "Watching Television without Pity: The Productivity of Online Fans." *Television & New Media* 9(1):24–46.

Barclay, Paris. 2016. "Statement from Directors Guild of America President Paris Barclay Regarding Entertainment Industry Diversity": *Director's Guild of America*. Retrieved December, 2017 (www.dga.org/News/PressReleases/2016/160125-Statement-from-DGA-President-on-Industry-Diversity.aspx).

Bentley, Jean. 2014. "'Orphan Black' Creators Dish on Tony the Trans Clone, Tatiana Maslany's Latest Masterpiece": *ScreenerTV*. Retrieved August, 2017 (http://screenertv.com/news-features/orphan-black-season-2-episode-8-tony-trans-clone-tatiana-maslany/).

Certeau, Michel de. 1984. *The Practice of Everyday Life*. Berkeley: University of California Press.

Costa, Daniela. 2017. "The Cast and Creators of Orphan Black Discuss the Show's Final Season": *Vice*. Retrieved August, 2017 (www.vice.com/en_us/article/gyp53b/the-cast-and-creators-of-orphan-black-discuss-the-shows-final-season).

Dershowitz, Jessica. 2017. "Orphan Black Star Says Season 5 Faces the Patriarchy Head-On": *Entertainment Weekly*. Retrieved August, 2017 (http://ew.com/tv/2017/06/09/orphan-black-season-5-cast-preview/).

Dessem, Matthew. 2018. "Amazon Cancels I Love Dick, Jean-Claude Van Johnson, and One Mississippi": Retrieved January, 2018 (https://slate.com/culture/2018/01/amazon-cancels-i-love-dick-jean-claude-van-johnson-and-one-mississippi.html).

Dowling, Amber. 2015. "Tatiana Maslany: Tony, Cages and Orphan Black Season 3—the TV Junkies": *TV Junkies*. Retrieved August, 2017 (www.thetvjunkies.com/tatiana-maslany-tony-cages-and-orphan-black-season-3/).

EW Staff. 2016. "Orphan Black Fans Can Create the Season 4 Poster—Exclusive": *Entertainment Weekly*. Retrieved August, 2017 (http://ew.com/article/2016/01/06/orphan-black-fan-art-poster-contest-season-4/).

Goldstein, Jessica M. 2015. "How Will Orphan Black Challenge Its Feminist Themes? 'Throw a Misogynist into the Mix'": *ThinkProgress*. Retrieved August, 2017 (https://thinkprogress.org/how-will-orphan-black-challenge-its-feminist-themes-throw-a-misogynist-into-the-mix-1471683f58d5/#.ktcd4pw44).

Hogan, Heather. 2014. "Fandom Fixes: Don't over-Dude It, 'Orphan Black'—Afterellen": *AfterEllen*. Retrieved August, 2017 (www.afterellen.com/tv/220749-fandom-fixes-dont-over-dude-it-orphan-black).

Holloway, Daniel. 2018. "'I Love Dick,' 'One Mississippi,' 'Jean-Claude Van Johnson' Canceled by Amazon": *Variety*. Retrieved January, 2018 (http://variety.com/2018/tv/news/i-love-dick-one-mississippi-jean-claude-van-johnson-1202667826/).

Ivie, Devon. 2017. "Pretty Little Liars Showrunner I. Marlene King Talks Fans and the Series Finale": *Vulture*. Retrieved June, 2017 (www.vulture.com/2017/06/pretty-little-liars-showrunner-i-marlene-king-on-the-finale.html).

Kinane, Ruth. 2017. "Riverdale Season 2 Will Go 'Darker and Deeper': Teases Camila Mendes": *ew.com*. Retrieved August, 2017 (http://ew.com/tv/2017/05/16/riverdale-darker-season-2-camila-mendes/).

King, Larry. 2002. "Interview with Mary Tyler Moore": *CNN Larry King Live*. Retrieved October 1, 2017 (www.cnn.com/TRANSCRIPTS/0205/08/lkl.00.html).

King, Marlene. 2014. "I Am Writer, Director and Producer Marlene King. You Might Know Me from Pretty Little Liars, Just My Luck, Now and Then, or Any Number of Different Projects. Ama!": *Reddit*. Retrieved August, 2017 (www.reddit.com/r/IAmA/comments/27prs2/i_am_writer_director_and_producer_marlene_king/).

Koblin, John. 2017. "Forget Ratings: Orphan Black Had the #Cloneclub": *New York Times*. Retrieved August, 2017 (www.nytimes.com/2017/08/10/business/media/orphan-black-cloneclub.html).

Loofbourow, Lili. 2015. "The Many Faces of Tatiana Maslany": *New York Times*. Retrieved August, 2017 (www.nytimes.com/2015/04/05/magazine/the-many-faces-of-tatiana-maslany.html).

Lotz, Amanda D. 2006. *Redesigning Women: Television after the Network Era.* Illinois: University of Illinois Press.

Lotz, Amanda D. 2017a. "Linking Industrial and Creative Change in 21st-Century US Television." *Media International Australia* 164(1):10–20.

Lotz, Amanda D. 2017b. *Portals: A Treatise on Internet-Distributed Television,* Vol. 9699689. Ann Arbor, MI: Michigan Publishing, University of Michigan Library. Retrieved August 2017.

Mason, Heather. 2017. "Thanks to Twitter, 'Riverdale' Fans Actually Helped Fix Clifford Blossom's Whole Wig Situation": *hellogiggles.com.* Retrieved August, 2017 (https://hellogiggles.com/reviews-coverage/tv-shows/thanks-to-twitter-riverdale-fans-actually-impacted-clifford-blossoms-whole-wig-situation/).

Penley, Constance. 1997. *Nasa/Trek: Popular Science and Sex in America.* New York: Verso.

Radway, Janice A. 2009. *Reading the Romance: Women, Patriarchy, and Popular Literature.* Chapel Hill: University of North Carolina Press.

Renée, V. 2013. "Director Edward Burns Looking to Twitter Followers for Feedback on Upcoming Film Project": *NoFilmSchool.* Retrieved August, 2017 (https://nofilmschool.com/2013/03/director-edward-burns-twitter-upcoming-film-project).

Ross, Dalton. 2014. "Orphan Black: The Creators Discuss Introducing Tony the Transclone": *Entertainment Weekly.* Retrieved August, 2017 (http://ew.com/article/2014/06/07/orphan-black-tony-transclone-creators/).

Telefilm Canada. 2016. "Telefilm Canada Feature Film Portfolio to Better Reflect Country's Greatest Asset—the Diversity of Its People": *Telefilm Canada.* Retrieved October, 2017 (https://telefilm.ca/en/news-releases/telefilm-canada-feature-film-portfolio-to-better-reflect-countrys-greatest-asset-the-diversity-of-its-people).

Thomas, Kaitlin. 2014. "Orphan Black's Creators on Their Newest Character, Being a 'Feminist' Show, and More": *TVGuide.* Retrieved August, 2017 (www.tvguide.com/news/orphan-black-new-clone-1082659/).

Thompson, Kristin. 2003. *Storytelling in Film and Television.* Cambridge, MA: Harvard University Press.

Thornton, Max. 2014. "Trans Men on TV: Orphan Black and Tony the Trans Bandit | Bitch Flicks": *BitchFlicks.* (www.btchflcks.com/2014/06/trans-men-on-tv-orphan-black-and-tony-the-trans-bandit.html#.WkliMt-nGUk).

Towers, Andrea and Jonathan Dornbrush. 2015. "'Orphan Black' Season 3: Are the Male Clones an Exciting Twist or Cause for Concern?": *Entertainment Weekly.* Retrieved August, 2017 (http://ew.com/article/2015/04/16/orphan-black-season-3-male-clones-debate/).

Tracey, Liz. 2015. "Will the Male Clones Ruin Orphan Black?": *Dame Magazine.* Retrieved August, 2017 (www.damemagazine.com/2015/05/04/will-male-clones-ruin-orphan-black/).

Vlessing, Etan. 2018. "How Canada Became a Springboard for Female Directors": *The Hollywood Reporter*. Retrieved February, 2018.

Zubernis, Lynn and Katherine Larsen. 2011. *Fandom at the Crossroads: Celebration, Shame and Fan/Producer Relationships*. Newcastle upon Tyne, UK: Cambridge Scholars Publishing.

INDEX

Note: Page numbers in *italic* indicate a figure and page numbers in **bold** indicate emphasis on the corresponding page.

CPSIA information can be obtained
at www.ICGtesting.com
Printed in the USA
LVHW081948111119
637000LV00012B/304/P